Southern Steam Swansong

The Final Years, 1964-67

Paul Cooper

www.crecy.co.uk

First published by Crécy Publishing Ltd 2017

A CIP record for this book is available from the British Library

Publisher's Note: Every effort has been made to identify and correctly
attribute photographic credits. Any error that may have occurred is
entirely unintentional.

ISBN 9781909328679

Printed Printed in Slovenia by GPS Print

Crécy Publishing Limited
1a Ringway Trading Estate
Shadowmoss Road
Manchester M22 5LH
www.crecy.co.uk

Picture Credits

Every effort has been made to identify and correctly attribute photographic
credits. Should any error have occurred this is entirely unintentional. Please
note I have shown the photographers initials for each credit. Photographers
are credited as follows: GPC for the author; KGV for Ken Vernon; JLMC for
John McIvor; RNT for Roger Thornton; RH for Roger Holmes.

Front cover:
'WC' No 34013 *Okehampton* has steam to spare at Waterloo at the head of
the 15.35 Waterloo–Weymouth in March 1967. Alongside, 'Crompton' D6546
at the head of an 8TC unit awaits departure on one of the recently dieselised
services. *KGV*

Back cover:
'WC' 34006 and 'BB' 34057 pause at Shepton Mallett on the LCGB's 'Farewell to
the Somerset & Dorset Route' special on 5 March 1966. *KGV*

CONTENTS

The author at Ropley, Mid Hants Railway, in 2017
with WC 34007 *Wadebridge*. PJC

Acknowledgments

The author would like to thank the following contributors to this book: Tim Crowley; Les Greer; Les Kent; Jim Lester; Jim Martin; Alan Newman; Bernie Knibbs; Geoff Burch; Kevin Robertson; John McIvor; Peter Cooper; Chris Jenner; Bob Leggett; Ian Simpson; Roger Holmes; Roger Thornton and Tony Twigg, without whom Ken Vernon's superb photos might well have been lost forever.

I would also like to acknowledge the role played by my family, from my grandfather first showing me glass plates of Adams 'T3s' he had taken at Romsey in 1910, through my parents' encouragement of my photography with some creative combination of Christmas and birthday gifts, to my wife and children who 'enjoyed' many a railway related diversion on a family holiday. Over the years long hours in the darkroom were tolerated as was more recently the time devoted to the tyranny of the scanner. And, finally, to future generations, as represented by my grandchildren, who are just being introduced to the joys of steam railways. Long may we keep the wheels turning for this unique combination of sound, sight, smell and speed that will continue to evoke such visceral emotions well into the 21st century, some 200 years after Messrs Trevithick and Stephenson started it all …

Abbreviations

Please note for the detailed captions, rather than repeat which type of Bulleid Pacific I am referring to, I have generally used the initials 'MN', 'WC' and 'BB' as below:

'MN'   'Merchant Navy' class

'WC'   'West Country' class

'BB'   'Battle of Britain' class

This is the final society-run steam railtour on the SR on 18 June 1967, which involved a trip to Weymouth via the Portsmouth direct route. Green Standard Class 5 73029, crewed by driver Lew Wooldridge and fireman Ray Bartlett of Guildford, makes a fine sight ahead of 'WC' 34023 *Blackmore Vale* in third-rail territory as the pair climb the 4 miles of 1 in 80 from Witley to Haslemere. It was a very hot Summer's day and many fires were set along the route that led to normal services being extensively disrupted. This incident left SR management with a sour taste towards steam working for the best part of 20 years thereafter. *GPC*

Introduction

Can it really be 50 years since that momentous year of 1967 when we witnessed the end of steam on the Southern Region (SR) of BR? I was 16 at the start of the year when Campbell died on Coniston Water in the January, the Six-Day war was raging in the Middle East in June adding 2d to the price of a gallon whilst the Beatles were counting holes in the Albert Hall, in November Harold Wilson talked about the 'pound in our pockets' as we faced our first currency devaluation for 20 years and the year ended with the breathalyser and the Hither Green disaster. Much has elapsed since then but for this book we will concentrate on the smoke-tinted spectacles as witnesses to the end of SR steam.

In the past I have penned and illustrated the occasional magazine article on the 5th/25th/35th and 40th anniversaries. However, to be able to produce a 176-page book this time rather than just a short article has been a real privilege and made possible by extensive use of previously unpublished pictures. Not only previously unseen, many are of the highest quality because they were taken on large-format Kodak Ektachrome slide film using a Rolleiflex 2.8F camera. Just to put this into context, the Rollei was a top-of-the-range German twin-lens reflex camera utilising a sharp F2.8 Zeiss Planar lens.

Whilst I was latterly using a Petriflex V 35mm SLR with F2 lens (which was pretty good for its time), the Rollei which cost £165 in 1964 (£3,000 in 2017) was giving an image size over four times larger than 35mm. The additional bonus has been the steadfast quality of Kodak's Ektachrome film that has remained stable over the past 50+ years. In consequence, some of the pictures yield a great level of detail with warm colour hues that you have to create digitally on modern cameras/iphones.

Now all this has been made possible by a gentleman called Ken Vernon. He had spent a lifetime working in the photogravure department at Sun Printers in Watford. I never knew him personally but we had a mutual contact. When Ken died in 2011, aged 83, he had an enormous collection of Bassett Lowke and Hornby locomotives plus a huge library of books and prints to dispose of. I assisted in this task and the photos were discovered at the end of the process. What was intriguing was that he had glass plates from 1946 to 1952 with copious notes as to what/where/weather/ exposure etc. Then there is a hiatus until 1964 when he bought the Rolleiflex but the irony is, that of the 3,000-plus Ektachrome images I obtained, there was only the occasional pencilled note (as to loco type, also sometimes the location and year) on the

Above: Ken Vernon's Rolleiflex 2.8F, a beautiful piece of engineering, purchased from Wallace Heaton in 1964 for £165. It is shown against a pair of Gauge 1 live steam Bulleid Pacific models made by Aster. *GPC*

Above: Ken Vernon holds a plate carrier in the photogravure department at Sun Printers in Watford, c.1948. *WRL Archive*

The author taking a rear view of 'WC' No 34023 *Blackmore Vale* at Winchfield on the 10.24 Waterloo–Weymouth (SO) on 3 June 1967. *PJC*

Wallace Heaton envelopes from the day they were processed. Fortunately, there was an accompanying ticket collection which gave some clues as to where he had been, along with a few programmes from the railtours he travelled on. So a great deal of detective work was necessary, including the wonderful Six Bells Junction website plus the texts mentioned in the bibliography along with the contemporary railway press – *Modern Railways*, *Railway World* and the *Railway Magazine*.

Ken's material is a mix of railtour photos with some interspersed action shots and I have tried to select them on the basis of quality, interest, relevance and timescale. Some are records of well-known events – eg the Somerset & Dorset closure tours – but they offer a different, quality take on what might be a familiar scene. Others show Eastleigh Works or some of the last workings at Bournemouth or over the Swanage branch. To try to balance this approach, I have also included the work of a further half a dozen contributors other than myself. Firstly, my good friend John McIvor (who now produces steam videos under the SVS titles and runs the excellent Nine Elms

Enginemen's website), Peter Cooper, who conveniently captured me here in the foreground of the picture above, plus two others, Roger Holmes and Roger Thornton, brought to me by my Managing Editor, Kevin Robertson. In addition I need to thank Les Greer and Les Kent for providing some traincrew and footplate shots. As the book was in preparation, I also took advantage of the very active Nine Elms Enginemens Association by asking John McIvor to post some sample pictures to try to identify different crews and incidents. This has resulted in some marvellous contributions from those half-century-old memories and a dialogue with some of the enginemen actually pictured. I am thankful to them all for letting me use these new photos. There are a few images that might be recognised from years ago but I believe they are worthy of repetition. For instance, my photo of two rebuilt Bulleid Pacifics meeting in Winchfield cutting was first used by Cecil J. Allen in *Railway World* in September 1967 and by publishers fairly regularly since that time...but no book on this era would be complete without this very fortunate shot.

The rationale of the book is to provide a celebration of the last three years or so of steam working with the photos illustrating a variety of locations to show steam in everyday use along with the many special enthusiast trains in those declining years. It is not intended as an authoritative study on the intricate workings of that time. This has been well covered by John Bird and Keith Widdowson in the past and added to by the monumental data management task achieved by Ian Simpson in his sister book *Southern Steam Operations 1966-67* that tabulates the final years' steam workings in splendid detail. The photos start with scenes from Eastleigh Open Day in August 1964 when Ken first got his Rolleiflex and then mainly go on to cover the years 1965/6/7. The last Summer steam workings to Exeter in 1964 are not included, though for interest I show my only picture with 'ACE' headboard below, but we do stray from the Weymouth route to some central and southeastern parts of the SR too. We pick up on some of the many railtours utilising 'foreign' locos and then continue to the section covering the last week with its tales of 100mph running. Inevitably as the steam pool diminishes, there are pictures of the same locos on different dates and at different locations. So, arguably the book is a bit of a 'Bulleidfest'. But we do have the differentiation between 'Merchant Navy' ('MN') and 'West Country'/'Battle of Britain' ('WC'/'BB') classes and also between original and rebuilt versions. However, it is surprising what diversity there was around at the end with Standard classes, including tank engines, and, of course, the ubiquitous 'USAs'. To these we can add the diversity of foreign motive power including 'A4s', 'A2s' and 'Britannias', a 'Hall', 'Black 5', 'K4' and the preserved 'A3'.

When this book starts, I am 14 years old with a railway interest that was ever present. It is perhaps exemplified by taking my first photo of an original 'Merchant Navy' on the 'Bournemouth Belle' when I was aged 7.

Camera upgrades followed progressively so that I had managed to get a 35mm Ilford Sportsman in 1963 with 1/200th sec maximum shutter speed. I upgraded this to a better version with 1/500th shutter speed in 1964, followed by a Taron Eyemax with a superb F1.8 lens in 1965 and finally a Petriflex V SLR for the last 18 months of steam. Most pictures were taken in black and white as it was cheaper, had a faster film speed and it was what the publishers of the day wanted. So it was not uncommon to have the Petriflex loaded with black and white film and then borrow my father's Agfa Silette for colour work. This was a reasonably successful combination as the second Petriflex body only came on 15 July 1967 in time for my Shap ventures that following week!

My only picture with 'Atlantic Coast Express' headboard shows 'Merchant Navy' *Channel Packet* storming through my home town of Farnborough in 1963 taken on my first 35mm camera (an Ilford Sportsman with max 1/200th sec shutter speed). *GPC*

Showing I was smitten early, this is my first railway photo, taken on a Box Brownie, of an original 'MN' on the 'Bournemouth Belle' in 1956/7 at Cove Bridge, just to the west of Farnborough. *GPC*

The author's 35mm SLR Petriflex V camera as used in 1966/7, with a selection of tour programmes, tickets and photos. *GPC*

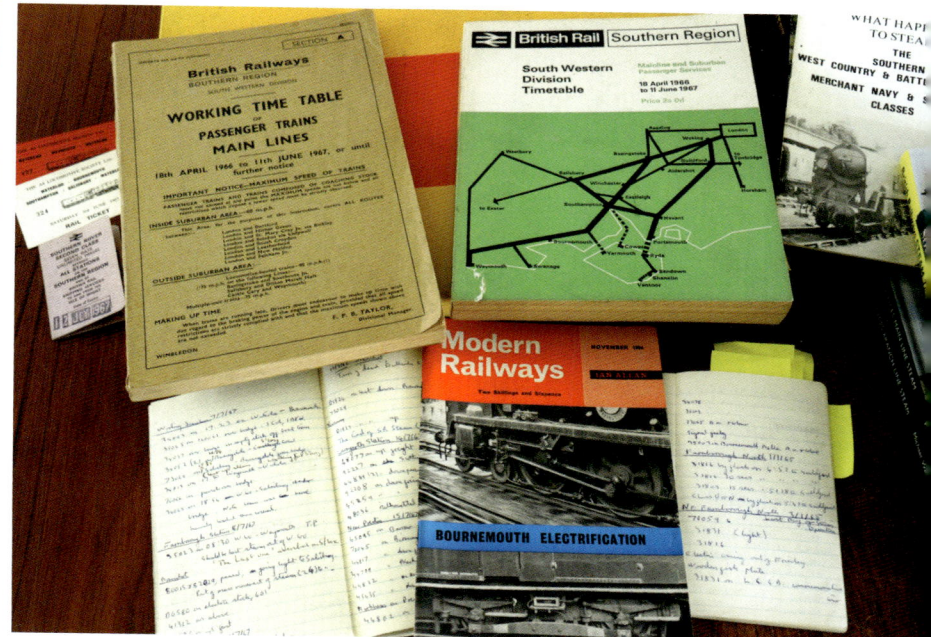

Working and passenger timetables with the *Modern Railways* November 1964 issue announcing the £15 million electrification scheme alongside contemporaneous photologs. *GPC*

I digress. I set off on a rail photo expedition to stay with family friends in York to capture the last of Eastern Region (ER) steam at Autumn half-term in 1964, the journey starting with a local Farnborough–Waterloo steam service before heading to King's Cross. I bought the November issue of *Modern Railways* at the W. H. Smith bookstall and its cover was a superb Colin Gifford close-up of Bulleid Walschaerts valve gear in motion illustrating the main feature, the announcement of the £15 million Bournemouth electrification scheme due for completion in early 1967. That represented the elimination of a 100% steam service in a little over two years and I resolved to record as much of the action as I could.

It is hard to recall what an intensive steam-worked service looked like but as you can see from the picture right at Deepcut there are three service trains in view in view in April 1965 whilst my records show I was linesiding two consecutive days during Summer 1964 and photographed no less than 55 steam workings!

There are three service trains (headed by Nos 35008, 35028 and 34052) in this view of Deepcut photographed in April 1965. *GPC*

The great limiting factor for me was mobility. I didn't start driving until the month steam ended so I was dependent on pushbike, cadging lifts or travelling by train. Even the last of these were limited by finances but I was fortunate in having an elder, driving brother who was an avid Southampton FC supporter. So many a time I got a lift south, sometimes being dropped on the Winchester by-pass next to the Shawford overbridge for linesiding and then needed just a single fare to Eastleigh or Southampton to explore more photo opportunities. And of course, when I could splash out on railfares, then some fine runs were made behind Bulleids such as 34013, 34024 and 35008 alongside some impressive station acceleration runs behind Standard Class 4s on Southampton locals. As far as specials were concerned, I couldn't afford them and, in any event, I preferred to photograph them rather than ride them. Ken Vernon, being some 20 or more years older, had no such fiscal constraints. So I have tried to achieve a balance between specials and service trains, statics and operational. I believe that the sheer technical quality of Ken's work justifies the large format reproductions. And, of course, filling a few gaps – eg Nine Elms and the very last up steam passenger working from John McIvor, some atmospheric fill-ins from Peter Cooper, Southampton surrounds from Roger Holmes plus the diversionary 'Alps' route and Upwey Bank from Roger Thornton – helps to tell the story more fully.

I hope you enjoy this celebratory volume as I am sure there are many of us, now retired, who have such vivid memories of those days – and just to give it some musical context related to vinyl that I still own, we start this review when The Rolling Stones 'It's All Over Now' tops the charts in July 1964 (coincidentally, as I write this listening to Desert Island Discs in late 2016, one of Bruce Springsteen's choices), go via the Kinks 'Lazin' on a Sunny Afternoon' during that languid, hot summer of 1966 and the laconic 'Waterloo Sunset' in 1967, to the release of 'Sergeant Pepper' the same year. I specifically recall chasing the 73029/34023 double-header special down the Portsmouth direct on 18 June 1967 in John McIvor's Buick Galaxy (yes, a Buick V8) and hearing the Beatles' 'A Day in the Life' for the first time on the last splutterings of the pirate radio stations. They were promoting the release of Sgt Pepper for 20 June. The music and locos that day set the world metaphorically and literally on fire – the performances were skin tingling and the embankments burning in the tinder dry conditions.

So, in summary, if it's not too grand a phrase, the underlying philosophy of this photograph-based book is to tell a familiar story using mainly new material. But it is also to feature some of the footplate crews when I have been able to identify them, mainly through the good offices of John McIvor as 'web/shedmaster' of the Nine Elms Enginemen's website. Many names are well known by the aficionados and of course anyone who ever got their hands on the regulator as a fireman or passed driver 50 years ago is going to be 70 years plus now. Many have helped in the formulation of this book and I would just like to show opposite a typical picture of a crew at Southampton, Reuben Hendicott and Les Greer, who you will see again mentioned later in this book.

Les kindly agreed I could publish his payslip for the last week of 1966. Gross, he earned £41, equivalent today to c.£800, for the week's work. But this entailed six-day working including his rest day with a total of 80 hours worked plus another 43 hours in mileage, extras and overtime. This was six return trips to Bournemouth or 212 miles per day and Les added that if he had worked the Sunday this would have added another 21 hours pay. Hard graft indeed!

In my only shot of a cab interior of a 'Merchant Navy', I have managed to grab the regulator of No 35030, in steam, in Salisbury shed on 18 March 1967. Excuse the Brylcreemed hair! GPC

Driver Reuben Hendicott (on the left) and Fireman Les Greer at Southampton after a run from Waterloo and back on 'WC' 34034 *Honiton. Les Greer Collection*

Fireman Les Greer's payslip from week ending 31 December 1966. *Les Greer*

Finally, I offer my thanks to two others. Firstly to Bob Leggett for lending me the individual locomotive repair cards for most of the light Pacifics, that emerged from an Eastleigh house clearance a few years ago. Given these are up to 70-plus years old, with the earlier locos starting in Southern Railway days with their 21C numbers inscribed, they are a wonderful piece of history. Some are reproduced later. And secondly to Ian Simpson who has attempted the mammoth task of documenting the detail of the last three years workings. He has provided the answer to many queries on where, when and on what...I look forward to seeing his published work *Southern Steam Operations 1966-67* on this topic too.

Paul Cooper
Winchester
March 2017

Eastleigh – The Works Open Day, 1964

Summer 1964 was the last 'proper' Eastleigh open day where the SR's finest workmanship could be displayed. The immaculate locos on display centred on 'Merchant Navy' 35007, 'West Country' 34037 and Riddles Standard 4 75016 and this was probably the last time locomotives were fully repainted. Eastleigh would continue to repair locos at the Light Casual/Intermediate stage until October 1966 – 'Battle of Britain'

34089 *602 Squadron* was the last outshopped loco but only nine months earlier there had been some seven Bulleids undergoing repairs. At the same time the finishing touches were being put to 'Schools' class 30926 plus 'M7' 30053 and ex GWR 2-8-0 2818, all undergoing some stage of restoration. I have also been fortunate in being able to track down the works repair cards for most of the light Pacifics and some pictures are included below.

Rebuilt Bulleid Pacific 'MN' No 35027 *Port Line* is undergoing a Light Intermediate overhaul in the works in September 1965 alongside a BR Standard Class 4. No 35027 was withdrawn in August 1966 having run 872,290 miles. *KGV*

A selection of Eastleigh Works loco cards for 'West Country' and 'Battle of Britain' locos. They cover most of the examples running in the last two years and provide a complete history from date entered service complete with SR 21C numbers for the pre-1948 builds. An absolute treasure trove of original information covering the lifetime of each locomotive with signatures of the relevant chargehands or foremen. *GPC*

Rebuilt 'WC' 34037 *Clovelly* has just received a Heavy Intermediate repair and been outshopped with a new coat of paint. Built in 1946 and rebuilt in 1958, she survived to the end of steam in July 1967, and ran a total of 810,658 miles. *KGV*

Eastleigh Works open day was a regular event for railway enthusiasts in the postwar years. It offered the opportunity for unconducted tours of the works to see everything from the working forge, through 'tyre shrinking', to the various states of dismantled locomotives being overhauled, be it Light Casual or Heavy Intermediate repairs, or general overhaul. The works occasionally overhauled other Regions' locos too, mainly those of Standard classes. In this picture taken on 5 August 1664 can be seen Standard Class 4 No 75016, which was built in 1952 and shedded at Nuneaton at the time of overhaul, and behind is Bulleid/Raworth 750V DC electric loco 20002, built in 1941. They were withdrawn respectively in 1967 and 1968. *KGV*

Following withdrawal of Eastleigh's steam crane in 1963, it was replaced with a Cowans Sheldon 30T diesel hydraulic unit, No DB965184, paired with its match wagon DB965184. The crane was in demonstration mode later in the day. Harry Frith, chief erecting shop foreman, who oversaw the last Bulleid repairs and the restoration of several locos (his name was attached to 'S15' No 30828), is seen leading a gang of men to the right of the picture. *KGV*

The 'Schools' class along with the surviving 'King Arthurs' and 'Lord Nelsons' were all withdrawn at the end of 1962. One member of each class was stored for preservation, though in the case of the 'Schools' class, two further locomotives were to escape the cutter's torch – 30926 *Repton* and 30928 *Stowe*. The latter was bought by Lord Montagu for the then Montagu Motor Museum at Beaulieu whilst 30926 was purchased by Steamtown Museum in Vermont, USA. Here 30926 is at the back of the works awaiting restoration on 5 August 1964. *KGV*

'Schools' class *Repton*, restored to Southern Railway livery, receives finishing touches in Eastleigh Work on 1 October 1966. In a remarkable piece of PR, I had written to the Works Manager that I understood the locomotive was being restored and would love to photograph it when complete. I received a letter inviting me to call to fix a time to visit. I think they were quite surprised when two teenagers walked into the works office, absolutely drenched following a 40 mile Lambretta ride though admittedly carrying full camera/tripod equipment. No 30926 was latterly repatriated to the North York Moors Railway. The 'M7' can be seen in the background and both locos were shipped to Gladstone Dock, Liverpool, on 18 April 1967 from Preston Park. *GPC*

Opposite: Another loco destined for Steamtown was 'M7' class No 30053. Again at the back of the works on 5 August 1964, having been withdrawn from Bournemouth in May of that year, she was under partial restoration at the time of 926's completion. She was subsequently repatriated to the Swanage Railway in the early 1980s. *KGV*

'Merchant Navy' Pacific No 35022, temporarily reduced to Atlantic 4-4-2 status, awaits re-assembly outside the works on 9 January 1966. Presumably with a problem on the leading axle, *Holland-America Line* was returned to traffic the same month but was only to survive a further four months – a quick demise from her immaculate state some six months earlier as will be seen later in the book. In the background is ex Great Western Railway (GWR) Churchward 2-8-0 No 2818 awaiting restoration for the projected Bristol City Museum. *KGV*

Fellow 'Merchant Navy' Pacific 35008 *Orient Line* is undergoing what is recorded as a Light Intermediate repair in September 1965. With wheelsets, cylinders, steam pipes and smoke deflectors removed, the locomotive appears to be in preparation for significant further running. No 35008 was to run to the end of steam in 1967 and, having been built in 1942, managed to run up 1,286,418 miles – though still a long way short of the original economic justification for the rebuilding process that assumed a life to 1975. *KGV*

West Country 34006 *Bude* undergoes a Light Casual repair in January 1966. Built in 1945, 34006 was the only example of the class that latterly ran with extended smoke deflectors (the other two examples losing them when rebuilt). Whilst taking part a few weeks later in the Somerset & Dorset (S&D) closure memorial runs, she was withdrawn in March 1967 having run the highest mileage of her type at 1,099,038 miles. *KGV*

Steam goes East

Most Southern farewells are confined to the former London & South Western Railway (LSWR) main line. It is therefore easy to forget that, whilst regular steam had largely disappeared in the early 1960s from the Central and Eastern divisions, there were some outposts of steam on cross-country services like Brighton–Portsmouth/Plymouth plus some of the branch lines. However, even this was very thin gruel by the time we get to mid 1965 (but see below). However, there were some notable specials, particularly over the Beeching-impacted branch lines such as the 'Cuckoo Line' to Eastbourne and the Horsham branch.

We start this section with the only service train in the feature. Steam had been all but eliminated along the south coast service but in the winter of 1965/66, the Class 33 'Cromptons' were not fitted with steam heating. Initially, steam operated from Chichester on these services but steam traction was reintroduced from Brighton on some services in January 1966 until the Summer timetable was introduced in the following May. Here Riddles Standard 5 73093 starts the 10.25 Brighton–Southampton service from the terminus in January 1966. No 73093 first entered service in 1955 and was allocated to the Southern Region in March 1965, first to Eastleigh and then to Guildford, where she survived until July 1967. *KGV*

Brighton station, somewhat modified from Mocatta's original design but which, along with the trainshed, was listed in 1973, makes a superb view bathed in afternoon winter sunlight. I doubt this photograph was entirely a matter of luck. It rates, in my view, as one of the all-time greats of the 'under the canopy' pictures at which Ken Vernon was particularly skilful. The angle of view, the light and the sheer interest within the picture make it stand out. In the background the majestic 'Brighton Belle can be seen, having arrived as the 11.00 from Victoria, whilst in the foreground are the recent BRUTE parcels trolleys that became universal over the BR network. The main subject is Maunsell 'N' class Mogul No 31866, which has just run in on a Locomotive Club of Great Britain (LCGB) special from Waterloo on 5 December 1965 that traversed the Horsham and Steyning branches. No 31866 was shedded at Guildford but had only transferred a year earlier – hence the lack of a shedcode – and would be withdrawn the following month. *KGV*

'Merchant Navy' class 35007 *Aberdeen Commonwealth* awaits departure from Brighton on a combined RCTS/LCGB 'Midhurst Belle' tour on 18 October 1964. This train had traversed a circuitous route via Ascot, Woking, Christ's Hospital, Midhurst, Pulborough, Littlehampton and Brighton Kemp Town, with a range of motive power. No 35007 was in fine fettle, having been one of the locomotives on display at Eastleigh open day back in August following a Heavy Intermediate repair. On this particular trip back to Victoria she was booked for 58 minutes (electric service trains were scheduled in 60 minutes) but she actually achieved start to stop in a shade over 56 minutes. *KGV*

The 'Q' 0-6-0s from 1938 were designed by Maunsell as powerful class of 20 4F locomotives. With a tractive effort of 26,000lb they were just 13% less powerful than Bulleid's rather austere 'Q1' class some four years later. Here 30530, with original elegant chimney rather than the Lemaître multiple-jet blastpipe fitted to other members, makes a rare appearance at Brighton Kemp Town terminus on an enthusiasts' special of 18 October 1964. The branch opened in 1869 but was closed to passenger services in 1932. Freight traffic continued to be handled up to 1971 and the tunnel under the town found refuge use during World War 2 as storage sidings for passenger stock overnight as Brighton was hit several times by Luftwaffe bombers emptying their load on the town after unsuccessful raids to London. No 30530 was withdrawn two months later and the class had been eliminated by June 1965. *KGV*

The 'Wealdsman' railtour on 13 June 1965 was an ambitious excursion with double-headed trains over recently closed Southern branch lines. Here, a contrasting pair of Moguls pause for a photo stop at Forest Row on the East Grinstead–Groombridge section before heading down the 'Cuckoo' Line to Polegate and Eastbourne. Maunsell Class U No 31803, a Guildford engine, was introduced in 1928 as a rebuild of the ill-fated 'River' class tank engine and survived into March 1966. Class N 31411, built as late as November 1933 at Ashford Works and similarly a Guildford loco, has had some 'TLC' and was to survive until April 1966. The 'Cuckoo Line's last steam passenger service worked the previous day and this tour was the last steam working over the 'Cuckoo'. *KGV*

The 'Vectis' railtour of 3 October 1965 proceeded from Chichester to Lavant on the closed line to Midhurst with 'Q1s' 33020 and 33027 'topped and tailed.' Here the special stands at Lavant station at the southern end of the branch opened in 1881. Passenger services were withdrawn as early as 1935 with freight withdrawn further north in 1953. Lavant, however, survived until 1968 and a further truncated line cut back south of the station for gravel workings survived until 1991. *KGV*

'West Country' 34002 *Salisbury* has worked the 'Vectis Farewell' tour into Chichester on 3 October 1965 and takes water whilst the train is handed over to 'Q1' 0-6-0s 33020 and 33027 to work the Lavant branch. *KGV*

Later in the day 34002 *Salisbury* was reattached to the train, to head to Portsmouth Harbour, where participants left the train to visit the Isle of Wight for a steam service to Ventnor. No 34002 was built in January 1945 and survived until April 1967. Originally scheduled for preservation as the oldest original Bulleid Pacific, she was supplanted by her more famous 'Battle of Britain' sister 34051 *Winston Churchill*. *KGV*

The 'Wealdsman' tour returned via the recently closed Horsham–Guildford route with double-headed 'Q1' 0-6-0s working the train all the way back to Waterloo. Bulleid's austerity freight locos were introduced in 1942 and were the most powerful of their type with a tractive effort of 30,080lb. Whilst not as elegant as their 'Q' predecessors, they incorporated Lemaître exhaust and multiple-jet blastpipe from new and were designed for ease of maintenance. The last examples, including Nos 33006 and 33027 illustrated here, survived until January 1966. Bathed in Summer evening light, they have paused at Baynards for a photo stop midway along the branch which had also closed the previous day, 12 June 1965. *KGV*

'WC' class 34102 *Lapford* survived until the end of steam and was the only original Bulleid Pacific active in the last week of SR steam operation. Here she is pictured at the buffer stops at London Bridge having worked the 'Surrey Downsman' special on 5 March 1967. I have included this shot as it is the only example I have of late steam at London Bridge. The period clutter makes for an overall view of railway working 50 years ago, with a collection of destination boards and even internal railway mailbags labelled 'London Bridge'. The train continued around to Victoria behind Standard 4 75077. *KGV*

The Veterans Bow Out

The last three years saw the diverse mix of Southern steam reduced to the Bulleid Pacifics and a number of Standard classes. The Moguls and 'S15s' suffered with the introduction of the Western Region (WR) diesel multiple-unit (DMU) service on the Basingstoke–Woking local services and the 'Qs'/'Q1s' were progressively eliminated from their local freight and engineers trains. The last 13 examples of the 'S15s', 'Q1s', 'Us' and 'Ns' were eliminated by June 1966. Remarkably the Adams '02s' of 1889 were the real veterans, retained for the Isle of Wight services that were cut back in early 1966 and closed for electrification at the end of that year.

Maunsell 'N' class Mogul 31411 pauses at Basingstoke with a Basingstoke-Waterloo local passenger service in September 1964. As we have seen earlier this locomotive was photographed subsequently in more pristine condition and managed to survive until April 1966, working the first of the Longmoor Military Railway specials on 16 April 1966 but withdrawn by the time of the re-run of the tour two weeks later. *KGV*

It's New Year's Day 1965 and on a crisp night at Farnborough North 'N' class 31816 pauses in front of the station signal box with a Reading–Redhill service on the last weekday service of steam operation. Then allocated to Redhill, following steam's demise she was re-allocated to Guildford and withdrawn one year later. *GPC*

The last day of steam working on the Reading–Redhill route was Sunday 3 January 1965. A Maunsell commemorative tour was scheduled and duly arrived behind a pristine 31831. However, although a Sunday, there were a number of service trains and here the ever-busy 'N' class 31816 hauls the 11.50 Reading–Redhill train along the Blackwater Valley with next stop Farnborough North. *GPC*

A timeless scene at Guildford on 21 April 1965 as 'Q1' 0-6-0 33006 simmers in the coaling yard adjacent to the station. Guildford was a fine repository of the older ex SR locos and only a few years earlier it would be common to see Drummond Class 700s here and the ubiquitous 'B4' 0-4-0 tank but regrettably these fall just outside our timeline. No 33006 was one of the last three 'Q1s' withdrawn from service in January 1966. However, she was retained in working condition specifically for a railtour duty in the New Forest and was not finally taken out of service until 3 April 1966. *GPC*

'Q1' 33018 heads a Ripple Lane (Barking)-Hamble oil tanker train through Guildford on 21 April 1965. This was a regular circular diagram worked by Guildford men that went empty down the Portsmouth direct to the Shell oil terminal at Hamble where oil was loaded and sent back up the main line via Eastleigh and round the North London line. No 33018 was transferred from Guildford the following month to Nine Elms and survived only a further three months to July 1965. *GPC*

Class U 2-6-0 No 31790 awaits departure at Guildford with a train to Redhill on a sunny winter's day in December 1964. This was the first of the 'U' class rebuilds of the 'K' class 'River' tanks withdrawn following the Sevenoaks disaster. Originally constructed in 1917, she was outshopped as a tender loco in 1928. Surviving until May 1965, she endured in one guise or another for almost half a century. *KGV*

The 'S15s' were another long-term survivor with a few examples making it through 1965 until the last withdrawal in 1966. Here Maunsell's 4-6-0 No 30839 is on railtour duty on the Waterloo–Woking leg of the 'Midhurst Belle'. However, this is no straight line special as the train has come via Ascot and Bagshot and is seen standing at Frimley, with an animated Station Master, before heading over the Frimley East curve at Sturt Lane Junction on the Waterloo–Bournemouth main line. There were through electric services over this route until the early 1960s but this was certainly the last steam train to use the route, and possibly the last train ever on 18 October 1964. No 30839 was a Feltham loco and survived until September 1965. *KGV*

Autumn 1964 saw the local Basingstoke–Waterloo services still very much steam operated. All classes of locomotives, bar the 'MNs', would be used on these trains. Here 'S15' class 4-6-0 No 30833 accelerates away from Fleet with a morning service to Waterloo on 17 October 1964. The services were taken over by ex WR DMU's at the start of the Summer timetable in June 1965 which coincided with the withdrawal of 30833. The class was introduced by Urie in 1920 but 30833 was from the later Maunsell batch of locos built in 1927 with six-wheeled tenders originally for use on the Central division. *GPC*

Mogul Class N 2-6-0 No 31811 starts her Basingstoke–Waterloo train away from Farnborough station under the magnificent signal gantry on 12 September 1964. This two-cylinder locomotive was built in 1920 and survived until May 1965. The LSWR electro-pneumatic signalling system was introduced in 1914 and was replaced under the electrification scheme with the new MAS system operated from three core signal boxes. The platforms at most intermediate stations would be lengthened to accommodate the new 12-car formations whilst the covered overbridge was to lose its canopy some 20 or so years later. (See page 76 for a 1967 contrasting view). *GPC*

Maunsell 'S15' class 4-6-0 No 30837 stands magnificently in Waterloo station awaiting departure of her train to Eastleigh Works via the Bentley/Bordon branches before heading over the 'Alps' on what is now the Mid Hants Railway on 9 January 1966. The train was planned for the following week but demand was so strong that an additional service was scheduled a week earlier. No 30837 was built in 1928 and was withdrawn in September 1965. She was reinstated specially from Feltham shed for these tours receiving a week's mechanical and cosmetic preparation beforehand. Owing to the grades on the Alresford route, the train was booked with six coaches though the load actually totalled seven coaches. *KGV*

The 'S15 Commemorative' tour was taken over by 'U' class 31639 at Bentley for the trip down the Bordon branch where there was an interchange for the Longmoor Military Railway that was still operating at the time. BR passenger services were withdrawn in September 1957. Here in bulled-up condition she runs around the train before the return trip. Built in 1928 as the first of the new 'Us' (rather than 'K' class rebuilds), and a Guildford engine for her last three years, she survived until June 1966. *KGV*

The second run of the 'S15 Commemorative' tour ran on a very cold, snowy 16 January 1966. The load had increased to eight coaches and whilst diagrammed for the 'S15' from Waterloo to Alton, the train was double-headed with 'U' class Mogul from Alton over the heavily graded route to Winchester Junction. Here 'S15' 30837 double-heads with 'U' class 31639 from Alton. On a personal note, I had planned to photograph the train approaching Bentley and then chase down the line for the double-headed, graded section. However such were the road conditions that the minor road we used near Bentley was also on a grade. It took three hours to dig the car out of the falling snow and get some traction (by my sitting in the boot) on the rear wheels of a V8 Buick (yes that V8 Buick again!) – not the best wheels to chase trains that day! *KGV*

In the far east of the SR there was a small outpost of steam at Ashford Wagon Works. Remarkably two Wainwright 'C' 0-6-0s from 1902, having been withdrawn from main service as Nos 31271 and 31592 in 1963, were transferred in departmental service as Nos DS240 and DS239 respectively. The latter survived to shunt wagons into the late Summer of 1966 following the transfer of two 'USA' tank locos (30065 and 30070) that were themselves to gain departmental numbers DS237 and DS238. The 'C' class DS239 was steamed for one last day on 8 October 1966 and is shown dropping her fire at the end of the day stabled alongside the two USA locos. Fortunately, having survived so long, there was a ready body of enthusiasts and funds to preserve her for the Bluebell Railway. *KGV*

Complete with wreath attached to tender and with the locomotive suitably chalked as 'Journeys End – The Last Trip, RIP', DS239 'C' class 0-6-0 is seen shunting the wagon works at Ashford on 8 October 1966. *KGV*

Opposite: The Isle of Wight network was cut back to the single line to Ventnor with the closure of the Smallbrook Junction to Cowes line in February 1966. The line remained steam worked until closure for electrification at the end of 1966, though not before the line had been truncated at Shanklin with the closure of the remainder of the line to Ventnor in April 1966. The postwar period was almost entirely the preserve of Adams '02' tanks that dated from 1889. Various Standard or Ivatt tanks had been considered for conversion to update the fleet but in the end the 'modernisation' was to be achieved by electrification and use of redundant London Transport tube stock dating from as early as 1925. This was progress on a budget!

In October 1965, run down but serviceable locomotives are seen in a dilapidated state at Ryde St Johns shed situated to the west of the station. The shed would remain open for a further year with locos even being repaired at the works on the other side of the tracks. W20 still carries its *Shanklin* nameplates whilst W31, *Chale*, has lost hers to have a chalk inscription 'Fireball' – presumably after the pre-Thunderbirds TV space series, Fireball XL5, instead. At closure all locos, except for W24, were taken to Newport for scrap though remarkably W27 was reported as being steamed on 18 April 1967 in order to shunt the line of redundant locos to enable scrapping to begin. *KGV*

The 'Vectis' railtour of 3 October 1965 pauses at Sandown on its way to Ventnor behind immaculate '02s' W24 *Calbourne* and W14 *Fishbourne*. The former loco had been through works recently and received a fresh coat of unlined black paint though lost its nameplates whilst the latter retained her full lining and nameplates. *Railway World* reported that by June 1967 the Wight Locomotive Society had raised £1,600 to purchase W24 *Calbourne*, three ex South Eastern & Chatham Railway (SECR) coaches and two ex London, Brighton & South Coast Railway (LBSCR) coaches – quite a package, even for £27,000 in today's money. *KGV*

The two Adams tanks have reached Ventnor and are uncoupled for watering and run round purposes before heading the special back to Ryde Pier Head. The Shanklin–Ventnor section closed six months later. W24 in the foreground survived until the end and was retained for engineers movements after the line closure. Consequently, she made it into preservation. W14, in the background, had the distinction of being the oldest working locomotive in the UK in 1966 and though present at the key events in 1966, failed to be preserved. She had operated the last Cowes line working, the last trains into Ventnor and the very last train from Shanklin on 31 December 1966. *KGV*

The Somerset & Dorset Succumbs

The Somerset & Dorset has had many tomes written on it and we will not cover its managed demise here. But, suffice it to say, it refused to adhere to the BR model closure plan and thereby gave enthusiasts the opportunity for some innovative workings. Not being ready for closure on the target date of 3 January 1966 that also coincided with the WR's objective of eliminating steam traction on the same day, it soldiered on for two more months until 6 March 1966, with the last service train being the 20.20 Templecombe–Bath Green Park behind Standard 4 tanks Nos 80043 and 80041. Several specials were run to supplement the local Ivatt tank workings and, as evidenced in one of the pictures here, at least one ex WR loco survived in steam beyond the planned termination date.

BR co-operated with the requested double-headed original Bulleid Pacifics to run one of the final weekend special workings. Two immaculate Pacifics, arguably over-manicured with the proliferation of white paint, were turned out for the trip accompanied by Nine Elms traction inspector Tim Crowley (today a sprightly nonagenerian). In December 2016 Tim told me he was on the footplate of 34057 and was advised by his driver to ensure he had a handkerchief to cover mouth and nostrils as there would be an abundance of sulphurous fumes in the single-bore Coombe Down tunnel, made worse by being on the footplate of the trailing loco. Accompanied by crystal clear early Spring lighting, nothing was to be seen quite like this again though two further specials were run the following day respectively by the Stephenson Locomotive Society (SLS) behind Standard 4 tank 80043 and '8F' 48706 and the Railway Correspondence & Travel Society (RCTS) with Bulleids 34057 and 34013 on part of the route. The last steam working over part of the route in fact took place a year later on 25 March 1967 when Ivatt 2-6-2 tank No 41320 worked the RCTS Hants & Dorset Branch Flyer to Blandford Forum.

Ivatt tank 41307 runs between A and B signal boxes at Highbridge. The A box originally controlled the S&D crossing to Burnham over the former GWR main line but closed in 1934 when replaced by C box the other side of the line. Here 41307 on 5 March 1966 runs round the train in readiness to return to Evercreech. *KGV*

Two Ivatt tanks, Nos 41307 and 41249, have arrived at Highbridge with the run from Templecombe via Glastonbury on the LCGB's 'Somerset & Dorset' railtour. *KGV*

Stanier '8F' 48309 pauses at Shepton Mallett with a full load of SR rolling stock on the 'Wessex Downsman' railtour on 4 April 1965. The '8F' ran the train from Bath Green Park to Bournemouth West before passing the train over to Bulleid Pacific 34051. This was one of several S&D commemorative runs and was planned when it was thought the line would close at the end of 1965. No 48309 was a Bath Green Park loco from August 1964 and withdrawn at the line's closure in March 1966. *KGV*

Bulleid's finest stand at Bath Green Park on 5 March 1966 waiting to start the return leg in the late afternoon sun. The curved roof of this fine station can be seen in the background whilst Traction Inspector Tim Crowley of Nine Elms takes an overview of the two original Bulleid light Pacifics, 'WC' 34006 *Bude* and 'BB' 34057 *Biggin Hill*. With a combined tractive effort of 55,000lb, the switchback grades will pose no problem for this mighty pair. No 34006 *Bude* entered service in August 1945 and, as we saw previously, was in Eastleigh Works only two months before this photograph was taken. She survived at Salisbury until March 1967. No 34057 *Biggin Hill* entered service some two years later in March 1947 and survived until May 1967 with 939,957 miles on the clock – no light Pacific exceeded 34006's total of 1,099,038 miles. *KGV*

'BB' 34057 *Biggin Hill* hauled the last through service train on the S&D – the 18.48 Bournemouth–Bath on Friday 4 March 1966. Here she is being serviced at Bath Green Park shed as one half of the Bulleid duo on 5 March 1966 whilst standing underneath the coal shute. She also double-headed 'WC' 34013 *Okehampton* on the last Bulleid working for part of the RCTS railtour the following day. Besides being an interesting general shed scene, the significant feature in this photograph is really the surviving ex GWR pannier tank, No 3681, devoid of numberplates. This loco should have been withdrawn with the elimination of WR steam on 3 January 1966 but survived until after the S&D closed on 6 March 1966 and was still in steam on 7 March. She was hauled dead by fellow pannier tank No 3758 to Bristol Bath Road for storage on 11 March 1966. Having been built in 1940, she enjoyed a longer life than the distinguished Bulleid guest visitors that day. *KGV*

Down the Line

With the WR having taken over the west of Salisbury workings in September 1962, SR management's plans for an intensive, high-speed steam service to the west of England in 1963 were never to materialise. The WR took the opportunity to 'rationalise' the parallel routes so the Summer 1964 timetable was to be the last year of intensive steam workings. The 'Atlantic Coast Express' had its final run on 5 September 1964 and the 'Warship' hydraulics were now to be the primary motive power to Exeter and the line subsequently singled and reduced to intermediate status. A plan to cascade 'Duchess' Pacifics from the London Midland Region (LMR) after their wholesesale withdrawal in September 1964 did not come to fruition, probably because of clearance issues combined with a general antipathy towards steam from the Raymond-managed WR whilst the South West main line had adequate numbers of locos, even if in variable condition. The main impact on steam services in mid 1965 was the introduction of off-peak local services operated by WR DMU shuttles between Basingstoke and Woking . However, all the main line services were either Bulleid (70 still in service at the end of 1965) or Standard 5 hauled. Locomotives were primarily stabled at Nine Elms, Eastleigh, Bournemouth , Weymouth and Salisbury.

Clearly the locomotive fleet was being wound down and although works visits continued right up to October 1966, these were not heavy repairs so no loco was reliveried. External condition was highly variable with the nadir perhaps being reached towards the end of 1966 but with a distinct improvement during early 1967 as several locos featured

regularly on special workings. Mechanical health was also extremely variable. Any serious faults led to withdrawal and quite a few locomotives were 'broken' towards the end through enthusiastic running. Nevertheless, many of the extant service locomotives were to put up some fine performances.

One outstanding run recorded by Winkworth was when Bert Hooker was allowed to let 'MN' 35023 *Holland-Afrika Line* loose on his last non-stop Waterloo–Salisbury run on 15 October 1966. In his autobiography he refers to the footplate inspector, Arthur Jupp, turning a blind eye and also to this being the first time he had worked with Fireman Dedman, as Hooker had switched his more remunerative Bournemouth working with his usual fireman Alan Newman (see later), to have a last 'crack' at the ton down the Salisbury route. Hooker claimed the fastest ever timing from Milepost 51 (Worting Junction, Basingstoke) to Milepost 81 (Tunnel Junction, Salisbury) – 20min 12sec– at an average of 89.9mph with 101mph at Andover and 82mph over Grateley Summit with eight coaches/275 tons. As Hooker says, 'I was able to give *Holland-Afrika Line* some more "stick" to get the train up to speed again. The faster the engine went, the more smoothly she rode, the running was surely effortless.' Winkworth confirms in his log that 102mph was achieved with

The WR takes over as 'Warship' D817 *Foxhound* heads an Exeter service and the local stoppers are operated by WR DMUs... but steam was still abundant in October 1965 when this was taken. *GPC*

Above and opposite: A contrast in condition as 'WC' 34004 *Yeovil* (above) enters Southampton in execrable state on 1 October 1966 whilst fellow 'WC' 34013 *Okehampton* (opposite) looks immaculate as she heads a track train at Fleet on 19 February 1966. She was earmarked for a special train the following day. The former was a Bournemouth loco whilst the latter was allocated to Salisbury, which generally had the best reputation for loco condition. *Both GPC*

25% cut-off and 240psi boiler pressure and adds 'no pushing the engine here and she rode magnificently – and quietly', achieving a net time of 71min 15sec over the 83.7 miles to Salisbury. Hooker was now regularly driving 'Warships' with 'Secondman' Newman but both were interchangeable between steam and diesel and Bert was to have his last fling on 'Battle of Britain' 34060 on the 08.10 Waterloo boat train on 26 June 1967.

The previous month to Bert Hooker's last non-stop Waterloo–Salisbury run, 35029 *Ellerman Lines* achieved 104mph at Hook with almost another 100mph recorded on the approaches to Farnborough on the up 17.30 Weymouth–

Waterloo on 6 September 1966. Superheater element failure occurred shortly after and a diesel took over at Woking. Mechanical failure also occurred to 35010 *Blue Star* with a blown cylinder near Woking the same week (see page 60) and to 35004 *Cunard White Star* earlier, at the end of 1965, with bent coupling rods and wrecked valve gear at Hook.

So, motive power problems by the end of 1966 were becoming critical. The remaining fleet was being held together with a patch and mend policy. Increased reliance was placed on the Bulleid light Pacifics and this then cascaded down to the Standard Class 5s. The Christmas parcels traffic that year

necessitated the reinstatement of ten locomotives (three Bulleids and seven Standards) to handle the increased traffic (see page 116). It doesn't seem likely that this brief respite lasted for more than three or four weeks with all locos being logged out of service soon afterwards. And as 1966 was drawing to a close, it was announced the new electrified service would not be ready in time for the start of the Summer timetable – it was now put back a month to 10 July 1967. Push-pull working would start on 12 December 1966 and the Brush Type 4s would be rostered for the 'Bournemouth Belle' from 1 January 1967. This brought home to every enthusiast the very imminent nature of steam's last fling – it would all be over in barely half a year. The year closed with the last rostered

steam-hauled 'Bournemouth Belle' worked by 34093 *Saunton* and 34047 *Callington* in the down and up directions respectively. Driver Porter of Nine Elms was on the regulator of the up working with 435 tons behind the drawbar and crested the 1 in 103 at Hinton Admiral at 60mph with 34047.

January 1967 saw the Southern still nominally retaining 130 steam locos in total, including 46 Bulleid Pacifics. The latter would be whittled down in time, such that by July they would total 25 including seven 'Merchant Navys' and two original light Pacifics. Concern was emerging that continuing delays to delivery of new stock and conversion of E50XX electric locos to the 2500hp electro-diesels might further delay steam elimination – initially scheduled for April and then June 1967.

According to November 1966 *Railway World*, contingency plans were being considered by SR management to borrow CIG and CEP electric multiple-units (EMUs) from the Brighton and Kent lines whilst the PUL and PAN sets would be reformed to handle Brighton line traffic pro tem.

Early 1967 also saw a pattern of remaining steam workings established until April. The introduction of the TC units had meant that some of the Eastleigh–Bournemouth locals had reverted to steam as the diesel power was needed for the new 8TC sets. The WR DMU service between Woking and Basingstoke was replaced by SR 2-EPB units pending the delivery of the new VEP units. *Railway World* also reported the arrival of the first REP power units along with more TC sets as modernisation progressed. With the introduction of the Brush Type 4s, it meant that from 2 January there were only seven down and eight up workings diagrammed for main line steam between London, Bournemouth and Weymouth. However, the main line still represented the most intensive steam passenger service in the UK though the third rail was expected to be energised to Bournemouth from 27 February. This meant that at the beginning of April the number of steam services would be further significantly reduced. Indeed, if the electric stock had been ready, they might have been all but eliminated then. In effect, it meant that between the 08.35 Waterloo–Weymouth and the 17.09 Waterloo–Salisbury (and even this service was lost to steam in June 1967) there were no main line steam workings diagrammed out of Waterloo. Most steam haulage numerically was rostered for the Eastleigh–Weymouth section with the main London hourly trains now given over to Brush Type 4s, electro-diesel/push-pull sets or EMUs. Fortunately, Fridays saw some extra services rostered for steam haulage from the capital but life was not going to be so straightforward for SW divisional management with the following three months witnessing numerous substitutions by steam. This often extended to the flagship 'Bournemouth Belle' with Brush Type 4 failures. I managed to photograph steam on the 'Belle' on seven occasions in 1967 and the total number of occasions must have been significantly greater. The last time the 'Belle' was worked by original Bulleid Pacifics in both directions was 4 May, with 'WC' 34023 *Blackmore Vale* and 'BB' 34057 *Biggin Hill* in charge respectively, but 5 July was to be the very last day of steam power on this flagship service.

On 4 March 'WC' 34004 *Yeovil* worked the last steam diagrammed York–Poole service in both directions but in the following weeks steam still appeared on these services, often making it onto steam-free WR territory as far as Reading. 2 April saw the dieselisation of the SR's last steam-worked branch line – Brockenhurst to Lymington –– where the last weekend's steam services were shared by Standard Class 4 tank 80152 and Ivatt tank 41312.

The last steam special down the Portsmouth direct route occurred on 18 June behind green Standard 5 No 73029 and original Bulleid Pacific 34023 *Blackmore Vale*. The extensive lineside fires resulting from this trip led to delays of the electric services that day and an antipathy towards steam on third-rail territory for many years.

Opposite: 'BB' 34077 *603 Squadron* starts the 11.30 Waterloo–Bournemouth service in April 1966. Introduced in 1948, 34077 was rebuilt in 1960 and was withdrawn from Eastleigh shed in March 1967. The locomotive achieved a lifetime total of only 745,642 miles. *KGV*

The WR had taken over the southern routes to and in the West Country at the end of 1962. Nothing much changed on the main line to Exeter immediately but Summer 1964 proved to be the last year of mass Southern steam haulage. To meet motive power demands there was potential to move the newly withdrawn LMR 'Duchesses' to the south to supplement the 'Merchant Navy' class but apart from any steam resistance there was the issue of platform clearances on these large locomotives. Hence, the WR proposed a cascade of 'Warship' hydraulic diesels, the first arriving in August 1964. Here in April 1966 an unidentified 'Warship' stands at the head of the 15.00 Waterloo-Exeter service alongside 'BB' 34066 *Spitfire* at the head of a down Salisbury service. *KGV*

Nine Elms had a significant allocation of varying Standard tanks in the last few years. These were mainly engaged on empty stock movements or on the Kensington Olympia services. At Waterloo in May 1967 an indescribably filthy Class 4 2-6-4 tank heads an empty stock working out of Waterloo. From the split number chalked on the running plate it appears to be 80140, one of 13 of the class allocated to Nine Elms, which remarkably survived until the end of steam. *KGV*

Original Bulleid Pacific 'WC' No 34102 *Lapford* stands at Waterloo on the evening of 23 September 1966 with a the 17.30 Waterloo-Bournemouth service. Although grimy, the locomotive appears to be in good mechanical condition with no steam seepage and with safety valves lifting. She gains an admiring audience in the form of a typical city gent replete with bowler hat, furled umbrella and leather case. A scene that would be gone in under a year though the city gent possibly took another 20 years to shed his uniform for the more brash style of the next generation of bracered brokers, bankers and civil servants. *JLMC*

Left: As perhaps this photograph and the previous one attest, Eastleigh MPD did not have a particularly good reputation for looking after the external appearance of its locomotives. They were not alone, of course, but most of the remaining sheds managed to turn out respectable looking machines towards the end. Here 'BB' 34088 *213 Squadron* awaits the 'off' on the 10.30 Waterloo to Weymouth service on 29 March 1966. Fast to Southampton and Bournemouth, the train would arrive in Weymouth 3hr 15min later. The loco would not be withdrawn for a further year. *GPC*

These four photos illustrate the working of the 'Bournemouth Belle' from Waterloo on 29 March 1966. Forming the 12.30 departure, the train consists of all-Pullman stock and runs in the same times as other fast Bournemouth services with only one intermediate stop at Southampton for water. The stock was stabled at Clapham Junction (departing 11.41), usually loaded to 10 cars (12 cars FO) and is hauled into Waterloo by Standard Class 4 tank 80143 as it passes sister engine 80145 on the neighbouring platform.

With the stock berthed in the platform awaiting Class 7 or 8 motive power, two Class 3 Standard locos, 82019 and 82029, are seen ready to proceed light engine back to Nine Elms having worked in empty stock previously on neighbouring platforms.

The 'Belle' was usually assigned a Class 8P 'Merchant Navy' with its extra power rating but here a very rough looking light Pacific 'BB' 34082 *615 Squadron* has been coupled up to the train ready for departure. Another Eastleigh loco, the engine was so dilapidated that the cab sheets were perforated and holed with rust. I suspect the overall mechanical condition was not top notch either. She was withdrawn less than four weeks later.

Finally, with a pristine rake of stock, the 'Belle' leaves on time with steam to spare. *All GPC*

We are fortunate John McIvor gained access to Nine Elms shed on 12 September 1966 and took the following six views. An almost dystopian post-industrial landscape is formed by Nine Elms shed yard and Battersea Power Station . The vast four-chimney structure by Giles Gilbert Scott dates from 1934 for the first two-chimneyed building whilst the second pair of chimneys was added in the 1950s. It ceased operations in 1983 but was listed and is currently being regenerated as housing and offices. In contrast, 'WC' 34004 *Yeovil*, a Bournemouth loco, could not be in worse external condition with only the bright coat of arms in the nameplate providing some relief from the grime. 34004 was to survive to July 1967 and found favour with the cleaner's polishing rag early in 1967 as will be seen later. *JLMC*

Opposite top left: Ash accumulates in the smokebox of any steam locomotive and Bulleid's Pacifics were no exception. The fireman is shovelling out the residue which needed to be done on a daily basis to avoid the familiar hot spot that could be seen on the lower part of the smokebox door when left to accumulate. It was not unusual for shed staff to shovel five or more smokeboxes per day with half a ton of ash at a time. *JLMC*

Above: 'BB' 34057 *Biggin Hill* has her fire raked over the ashpit at Nine Elms. The proximity of the shed to the council flats can be seen clearly. It must have been a relief to residents when the Covent Garden Market Authority took over the site post the elimination of steam. *JLMC*

Left: An original 'WC' Pacific receives oil to the eccentric crank of the centre driving wheel. The structure of the 'solid' Bulleid Firth Brown 6ft 2in driving wheels can be seen here. Though solid 'boxpok' wheels were widely adopted in the USA on locomotives such as the New York Central 'Hudsons' and 'Niagaras', Bulleid was the only Chief Mechanical Engineer to adopt their widespread use both on his Pacifics and 'Q1' Austerity locos. *JLMC*

Rebuilt Bulleid Pacific 34090 *Sir Eustace Missenden* basks in the Autumn sun under cover in Nine Elms shed. Named after a former Chairman of the Southern Railway, this Eastleigh loco remained active until the end of steam. This location achieved some fame as the renowned artist David Shepherd undertook several of his canvases here depicting the dying, grimy days of steam in 1966/7. *JLMC*

'MN' 35010 *Blue Star* stands forlorn in Nine Elms the previous week having suffered a catastrophic failure with the destruction of its offside cylinder, perhaps from excessive priming, whilst working an up fast train between Walton and Hersham. The locomotive had apparently received some attention to pistons and cylinders at Guildford shed the previous day. Needless to say, withdrawal followed immediately, though not without 35010 having covered a cumulative 1,241,299 miles. *JLMC*

Rebuilt 'WC' 34098 *Templecombe* heads the 13.30 Waterloo–Bournemouth service through Vauxhall on 20 March 1967. The office blocks to the rear hugged the curve on the approaches to Waterloo but there was still sufficient space for the photographer to capture the Palace of Westminster and Big Ben in the background. No 34098 was delivered new into BR ownership at the end of 1949 but did not quite make it to the end of steam, being withdrawn in June 1967. *JLMC*

'WC' 34013 *Okehampton* is framed by the canopies of Vauxhall station in the Spring afternoon sun as she heads south with the 15.35 Waterloo–Bournemouth service on 11 March 1967. This locomotive was one of the most frequently observed in the dying months of steam and obviously had a good reputation for reliability. Shedded at Salisbury, she was a regular on the early morning and evening commuter services and was to survive until the end of steam. *GPC*

Views from a train. It is 11 March 1967 and I am heading for one of my occasional trips to London. In fact, twice in that month I was hauled by rebuilt 'WC' 34013 *Okehampton* to Waterloo. On the first occasion it was on the morning commuter service from Farnborough but on Saturday 11 March the local service was a DMU so I decided to connect into the semi-fast 08.46 Bournemouth–Waterloo at Woking. This was always a fascinating train, always a Bulleid Pacific and generally only loaded to four coaches. So, occupying the rear coach to try to get the benefit of the curvature approaching Waterloo, I waited for opportunities to get a few photos. Firstly on the approaches to Surbiton I caught 'MN' 35012 *United States Line* heading the 11.30 Waterloo–Bournemouth. Then, running through Clapham Junction, you can see the curvature through the station, the odd enthusiast on the station platform and one of the overbridge signal boxes spanning the tracks. Finally, as we near Waterloo, 34013 meets one of the SR EPB units on a suburban service. *All GPC*

Class 4 Standard 4-6-0 75077 stands at Kensington Olympia with the Victorian facades of the terraced houses of Addison Road in the background. The Motorail open wagons servicing the inter-regional services at the terminal there can also be seen. Designed by Robert Riddles, 75077 entered service in December 1955 and survived as an Eastleigh-allocated engine until July 1967. Having lost her original numberplate she became the beneficiary of Eastleigh fitter Ron Cover's handicraft skills when he affixed a painted metal replacement, as he did to several other locos. Here she is at the head of the 'Surrey Downsman' railtour bound for Tulse Hill on 5 March 1967. *KGV*

'WC' 34037 *Clovelly* heads 17.30 Waterloo to Bournemouth service through Raynes Park in the Summer of 1966. The loco still has nameplates attached and was allocated to Nine Elms at the time. Raynes Park retained its distinctive LSWR era signal box, having not been the beneficiary of the art deco style SR modernisation of the 1930s as seen at Wimbledon and Woking. *KGV*

'WC' 34034 *Honiton* was delivered to the Southern Railway from Brighton Works in July 1946 and rebuilt in August 1960. Latterly allocated to Eastleigh and Nine Elms, here she heads the 09.30 Waterloo–Bournemouth service in Summer 1966 through Surbiton. *KGV*

'BB' 34052 *Lord Dowding* has lost her nameplates by the time this photo was taken in late Summer 1966. She is seen passing the art deco style ex Southern Railway type 13 signal box at Wimbledon (opened in 1948) with a Waterloo–Salisbury service. By this time there were a number of morning and evening commuter services to Salisbury though occasionally steam would work as far as Salisbury on a Waterloo–Exeter service deputising for a failed 'Warship' diesel. *KGV*

No 77014 first entered service at Darlington in July 1954. A Riddles designed Standard Class 3 2-6-0, the locomotive was transferred to Guildford from Northwich in April 1966, having received an overhaul only the previous year. Her transfer was possibly the forerunner of several such to help handle the engineering trains for the Bournemouth electrification and provide replacements for the soon to be eliminated SR Moguls and 'Q1s'. In fact, only the one transfer was made and, as we shall see, 77014 was active to the end, admittedly away from her Guildford home base. Being unique, she was in demand for railtour duties too and here is seen just catching the Winter sunlight at Kempton Park with the 'South Western Suburban' railtour on 5 February 1967 – and again replete with a Ron Cover numberplate. *KGV*

Maunsell's elegant 4-6-0 'S15' class can be seen to full effect in this study at Woking station in October 1964. Introduced in May 1936, 30839 did not quite make 30 years, being one of the last two in the class to be withdrawn in September 1965. The other loco, 30837, was reinstated in January 1966 for the railtour workings commemorating the class. *KGV*

Much has been written about this famous train. 'Battle of Britain' 34051 *Winston Churchill* was fortunately still in service at the time the great war leader died, having been through a light casual repair at Eastleigh in December 1964. Churchill had expressed a wish to be buried near the family Blenheim Estate at Bladon, and to reach there by train from Waterloo. The locomotive was prepared and the crew of Lou Hurley and James Lester were hand-picked to drive the Bulleid Pacific. Jim recalls that eking out the water supply to reach Oxford shed was a major task, as was avoiding the safety valves lifting whilst in Waterloo station. 'BB' 34064 *Fighter Command* was held as a reserve locomotive. I recall watching the funeral service on TV and little did I know that 30 years later I would be occupying a Thameside office that replaced those saluting cranes. At the point the cortège unloaded from the barge, we left home to reach Binfield, just outside Bracknell, to photograph the passing special on 30 January 1965. James Lester in his book *Southern Region Engineman* states: 'On the train the engine performed as well as she looked.' No 34051 was withdrawn later in the year in September but had effectively auditioned herself into preservation. Note the special 'V' headcode, more normally associated with a breakdown train, but in this case paying homage to the Great Man's characteristic 'V for Victory' sign. *GPC*

Opposite: A quick diversion to Guildford is warranted by this magnificent shot of 'BB' 34052 *Lord Dowding* on a Southern Counties Touring Society (SCTS) tour. Whilst the locomotive has lost its plates, at least it has also lost the plateholder that rather marred the elegance of the locomotive when left attached to the running plate. The train started from London Bridge and 34052 took over the train at Wimbledon to Eastleigh and Salisbury. Here, on 9 October 1966, she has stopped for water and is in the hands of Guildford crew Driver Wattleworth and Fireman Earle. A Southern 2BIL unit sits on Platform 3 providing a period feel to the picture. *KGV*

16 October 1965 was a sunny Autumn day. The banked curve at Pirbright Junction combined with side lighting provided the right conditions for an action shot of 'MN' 35003 *Royal Mail* at the head of the down 'Bournemouth Belle'. Note the classic smokedrift that rebuilt Bulleids produced over the front of the smokebox but then was lifted clear by the smoke deflectors. The conductor rail is newly installed on the fast line as is the ballast and continuous welded rail. Fast to Southampton, the train was travelling at 80/85mph at this stage. No 35003 was introduced in 1941, rebuilt in 1959 and was operational in the last week of steam. *GPC*

'WC' 34102 *Lapford* is seen entering Deepcut on 16 October 1965 hauling the three-coach 12.39 SO Waterloo–Basingstoke service. This train was fast to Woking and unusually utilised the down fast track, switching to the slow line at Farnborough for all stations to Basingstoke. No. 34102 was to survive until the end. *GPC*

Further down the route the four-track main line runs in the appropriately named cutting at Deepcut and makes a magnificent sweep towards the short four-portal tunnel that runs beneath the Basingstoke Canal. Here 'BB' 34064 *Fighter Command* heads the 12.35 Waterloo–Weymouth on the down fast. This locomotive was uniquely (for a Pacific) fitted with the Giesl ejector, invented in 1951, the oblong shape of which can be seen from this high-level picture. Locomen awarded high praise to the engine which gave a coal saving of 8% (when fed the correct grade) and a power output increase potentially up to 20%. The locomotive also had the privilege of being the 1,000th engine constructed at Brighton, having been completed in July 1947. She was withdrawn less than one month after this picture was taken having run a total of 759,666 miles. *GPC*

Above: The 'Bournemouth Belle' rounds Pirbright curve on 5 March 1966 behind 'MN' 35013 *Blue Funnel*. No 35013 was built in 1945 and was one of the early rebuilds in 1956 and survived until July 1967. *GPC*

The sun just catches 'MN' 35005 *Canadian Pacific* at the head of the 'Bournemouth Belle' on 24 April 1965 at Deepcut. The following month, on 15 May 1965, she achieved 105mph on the descent to Winchester whilst hauling the 21.20 Waterloo–Bournemouth with Driver Hooper and Fireman Wilson but also, perhaps surprisingly, with a traction inspector on board. The locomotive was introduced in January 1942 and withdrawn in November 1965. She was rescued from Barry scrapyard in 1973 and returned to the main line in the 1990s. *GPC*

The omnipresent 'BB' 34052 *Lord Dowding*, but this time in her full pomp complete with nameplates and a light dusting to her paintwork. Pictured under the central arches of the five-arch span at Deepcut, this magnificent bridge supported a single-lane road above. No 34052 is at the head of the 11.30 Waterloo to Bournemouth service on 30 April 1966. She was one of six locomotives named after World War 2 leaders, of which three served in the Royal Air Force. Dowding was head of Fighter Command during the Battle of Britain in 1940. *GPC*

On the west side of Farnborough station on 6 October 1966, there is much activity related to the electrification programme. Besides berthed hopper wagons, 'BB' class 34066 *Spitfire* hauls a rake of empty hoppers, the 14.02 Woking to Salisbury. It was unusual to find a Bulleid Pacific on freight working; when it did occur it was mainly on these ballast workings. No 34066 was famously involved in the Lewisham Disaster in 1957 but was repaired and restored to traffic. Entering service in 1949, she was withdrawn in September 1966 and only managed a lifetime mileage of 652,908. *GPC*

Opposite top: Rebuilt 'WC' 34001 *Exeter* hurries the 'Cunarder', a Southampton Docks-bound boat train, near Sturt Lane Junction, on 9 April 1965. It was not unusual to have multiple trains on the same day for several ships berthed in Southampton at any one time. This continued right up to the last week of working. No 34001 was the first of the 'West Country' class completed in June 1945. Rebuilt in 1957, 34001 survived until the end with almost 1.1 million miles on the clock. 1965 was the last year that the SR stopped recruiting cleaners as the start point for the driving grades so this Nine Elms loco along with many others was in good external condition (as were most of the locos photographed that day). As we have already seen, 1966 was going to deliver rather different results. *GPC*

Bottom: The view from the A325 Portsmouth Road bridge over Farnborough station was an interesting one. Besides a clear view East towards what is known locally as Monks Bridge (connecting Farnborough Abbey to the Convent), the site was also the HQ of the Railway Enthusiasts Club in the days when memorabilia could be safely left outside. In fact, the 'Devon Belle' smoke deflector side name was 'borrowed' by local students for their ragweek in 1964 but was safely returned. Long demolished, the site became offices in the early 1970s. 'WC' 34004 *Yeovil* is seen at the head of the Warwickshire Railway Society tour to Swanage and Weymouth on 11 June 1967. *RNT*

'MN' 35030 *Elder Dempster Lines* with nameplates restored has been thoroughly prepared for an unusual special, 'The Dorset Limited', originating from Weymouth on 3 June 1967. The photo shows 120 years of history. The separation of the up and down lines at Farnborough is marked by a grass bank that was originally the down platform before the line was quadrupled. The station was opened in 1838 and rebuilt in 1903 as quadrupling progressed towards Basingstoke. All lines are shown electrified and relaid whilst Farnborough has lost its magnificent up and down signal gantries supporting the electro-pneumatic semaphore system from 1914. Platforms have been extended in standard white concrete in order to ensure 12-coach formations can be accommodated. Contrast the picture on page 35 from less than two years earlier. *RNT*

It's 25 June 1966 and I had just obtained my first 135mm telephoto lens for my 16th birthday. On its first trip out, I was fortunate enough to capture a number of steam workings through Farnborough station that Summer Saturday. Here 'WC' 34101 *Hartland* is at the head of the 'Bournemouth Belle' as she hustles her load on the cambered down fast line. In the background is the dome of St Michael's Abbey with its Benedictine order of monks and the mausoleum of the 1870-exiled Bonaparte family dynasty, Emperor Napoleon III, Empress Eugenie and their son, killed in the Zulu Wars. No 34101 was withdrawn less than a month after this photo was taken having entered traffic as late as February 1950 with only 568,479 miles to her record – barely run in, in railway terms. *GPC*

Mogul 2-6-0 31803 of the rebuilt 'U' 'River' class shunts Farnborough yard on 6 October 1965. This used to be a daily occurrence on local pick-up duties but became more frequent with the occasional engineers trains that were berthed in the yard. The Charringtons coal distribution facility can be seen on the right whilst 31803 is reversing onto a rake of low wagons under the watchful eye of the yard shunter. The fireman is demonstrating his balancing skills by shovelling coal forward whilst on the move. No 31803, with her Guildford shed name chalked onto the buffer beam, survived until March 1966. *GPC*

Admittedly not a steam picture but a rather interesting one nonetheless, taken 6 October 1965. Here 'Crompton' Type 3 (Class 33) D6548 hauls a freight train on the down slow line past 'Hymek' Type 3 (Class 35) D7021 at the head of yet another train of ballast empties. A fine period piece of BR green diesel liveries. Note the pile of third rail insulators in the foreground. *GPC*

'Crompton' Type 3 D6503 shunts coal wagons in the yard at Farnborough whilst Peckett tank 0-4-0 named *Invincible* wends its way into the yard having traversed the streets of Farnborough with its load of empty mineral wagons. This was virtually a daily working and survived the end of main line steam until April 1968. Coal was required to feed the boilers at the nearby Royal Aircraft Establishment thus requiring these regular visits. The three-mile line was constructed by German POWs in 1916 and closed when the boilers converted to oil. *GPC*

Whilst busy photographing the train movements in Farnborough Yard, the foreman of these gangers asked me to take a picture of the group and to send him a copy. This was duly done but I'm afraid I have no names for the men depicted. Both pictures were taken on 29 October 1965. *GPC*

With engineering possession of the main line frequently leading to closure between Pirbright Junction and Basingstoke as whole sections were relaid, through services to the south were often diverted on Sundays either down the Portsmouth Direct or via the 'Alps', the Alton–Winchester route that opened in October 1865. Here an unidentified Class 33 diesel and rebuilt 'WC' are depicted passing Aldershot signal box on the 09.30 Waterloo–Bournemouth service on 13 June 1965. *RNT*

An unidentified Standard Class 5 4-6-0 double heads 'BB' 34077 *603 Squadron* away from Alton to start the climb over the 'Alps' towards Alresford on the 09.30 Waterloo–Bournemouth on Sunday 24 April 1966. The train would regain the main line at Winchester Junction. *RNT*

The new image is emerging as BR's corporate blue/grey livery finds its way onto Mk1 rolling stock. Alternating with the SR green that remained on the Bulleid stock until withdrawal, this does look rather like motive power overkill on the 08.46 Bournemouth–Waterloo semi-fast. This working ran 15min behind the 'Royal Wessex' but stopped all stations to Basingstoke. A designated 8P locomotive for a four-coach train weighing less than 150 tons is likely to have encouraged some enthusiastic working. Here the crew of 'MN' 35013 *Blue Funnel* hurry her load through Bramshot, near Fleet, on 14 February 1967 knowing they face a clear road until they reach Woking. No 35013 was built in 1945 and was an early rebuild in 1956. She lasted till July 1967 and clocked up over 1.1 million miles. *GPC*

In the same spot on the same day, but approaching from the opposite direction, 'MN' 35030 *Elder Dempster Lines* is at full pelt with the 11.30 Waterloo–Bournemouth. These two pictures show the straight stretch of track often referred to as the 'greyhound stretch' that gave crews essentially level, straight track for the Farnborough–Basingstoke section of the main line. In the up direction locomotives were usually starting to be eased at about this point to prepare for the cambered curve through Farnborough to be taken in the low 80s. However, there is an instance recorded of 'MN' 35012 passing the station at 89mph in 1965 in the hands of Driver Hooper and another occasion recorded of 96mph behind 35029. *GPC*

Above: 'BB' 34087 *145 Squadron* rushes the down 'Bournemouth Belle' (having lost its Pullman brake ends) on the 'greyhound stretch' on 15 April 1967. The previous month, on 7 March, 34087 crewed by Driver Bill Anderson and Fireman Les Greer broke the informal record for breasting Roundwood Summit, 11 miles at a continuous 1 in 252 from a Winchester start, at 85mph whilst hauling the 19.38 Bournemouth–Waterloo. And there were more high-speed performances to come. *GPC*

Standard Class 4 4-6-0 75079 hurries along the 12.39 (SO) Waterloo–Basingstoke stopping train on the approaches to Fleet on 4 June 1966. Introduced to service in January 1956, she was the last example of the class and withdrawn from Eastleigh barely a decade later in November 1966. *GPC*

It is early 1967 and this shot fortunately worked first time. 'WC' 34019 *Bideford* is caught centre frame and there's no extraneous road traffic to block the view on this country road near Bramshot. The view remains today but the road has become a footpath as replacement feeder roads to the M3 were built and its main use to service the National Gas Turbine Establishment at Pyestock (where all the test work on the Olympus engines for Concorde took place in the mid-1960s – my father was the test cell design engineer and despite a career in aviation retains a fond interest in matters steam at the age of 97) was displaced following its closure. Reverting to an older technology, the filthy 'West Country' heads the 11.25 Weymouth–Waterloo on 14 February 1967 and was withdrawn one month later with a relatively low mileage of 701,316 for a 22-year-old locomotive. No 34019 was the last steam locomotive to work the Exeter route, this occurring on a special working on 13 November 1966. *GPC*

Opposite top: As late as 4 June 1966 the SR could still turn out an immaculate locomotive and train. Here rebuilt 'WC' 34026 *Yes Tor*, a Salisbury engine since 1960, heads the down 'Bournemouth Belle' near Fleet. Her sleek lines are shown to good effect and perhaps enhanced by only having a plain nameplate attached with no shield embellishments. The full Pullman rake still remains in use at this date with no BR corporate blue/grey brake ends to detract from the scene. No 34026 only survived a further three months with a life of just over 20 years and a mileage of 916,244. *GPC*

Bottom: To the west of Fleet station one of the magnificent full-width signal gantries is shown just a few months prior to dismantling. Original 'WC' 34015 *Exmouth* is on the down slow line heading a very mixed rake of rolling stock on the evening 17.41 Waterloo–Salisbury commuter train on 14 June 1966. No 34015, a Salisbury engine, was withdrawn in April 1967 after completing 903,245 miles. *RNT*

Opposite top: A little further down the line a year later, on 30 June 1967, the signal gantry has gone and the main line is being operated under the newly installed multiple-aspect signalling (MAS) operated from Basingstoke signal box. Rebuilt 'BB' 34087 *145 Squadron* hauls a complete rake of non-SR stock on the 17.23 (FO) Waterloo–Bournemouth service. Notably, the previous day 34087 achieved 95mph in the hands of Driver Reuben Hendicott through Wallers Ash and 91mph through Winchester Junction on a down working. On the return up working with Driver Shepherd of Eastleigh, 92mph was achieved at this west of Fleet location on the same day. Both trains were in excess of a 420-ton load comprising 12 vehicles! Built in December 1948, 34087 survived until the end, retiring with 704,638 miles on the clock. *GPC*

Bottom: On Friday evenings in the Summer there were scheduled additional boat trains for the Channel Islands traffic for Weymouth. This placed some pressure on a declining number of serviceable Pacific locos. Consequently, the Standard Class 5s tended to be seen on fast traffic work on these days. Here a de-plated 73043, carrying the incorrect headcode, hurries the 17.23 (FO) Waterloo–Bournemouth, first stop Winchester City, towards Hook on 26 May 1967. Built in 1953, 73043 was transferred to the SR at the end of 1962 and was a Nine Elms loco for its final year of working. *GPC*

There follow a number of photos in broadly the same location, the Winchfield overbridge being a key identifier. This area provided several convenient bridges to gain a good photographic vantage point whilst access to the track was easily achieved in those more liberal days. There was also the advantage of seeing the last of steam on the fastest stretch of steam-worked track on the whole BR network. Here, taken from the high bridge, rebuilt 'WC' 34013 *Okehampton* heads through Winchfield cutting with the 17.23 Waterloo–Bournemouth(FO) on 16 June 1967. *GPC*

This view looking west under the bridge shows 'BB' 34056 *Croydon* with a complete rake of Bulleid and BR Mk1 stock in SR green livery as she heads the 09.25 Weymouth–Waterloo train through Winchfield cutting on the hot Summers' day of 20 August 1966 (I was on the Isle of Wight lineside that day). Allocated to Salisbury, 34056 was to survive until May 1967. *RNT*

In Summer evening light 'WC' 34093 *Saunton* pounds along the straight and level track between Hook and Winchfield on 27 May 1967 at the head of the additional 16.00 Channel Islands Weymouth–Waterloo service. The power and speed of the locomotive is emphasised by use of a telephoto lens at a low angle with a slight pan of the camera. An Eastleigh loco, 34093 was to be active until the last week. *GPC*

It is 10 June 1967 and just one month of steam working to go. Summer Saturdays even at this late stage seemed to offer increased opportunities to witness steam working at its best. The unusual could still occur as here a now immaculate 'WC' 34021 *Dartmoor* heads the 10.00 Waterloo–Exeter, covering for a failed 'Warship' diesel. Steam would come off at Salisbury but this may well have been the last occasion steam substituted on these services. No 34021 remained a Nine Elms loco to the end so it is quite likely that her pristine condition was achieved with some outside help given the lack of cleaners and poor working conditions prevailing by then. *GPC*

By way of contrast, just four months earlier a filthy 'WC' 34021 *Dartmoor* is seen at the head of the 08.46 Bournemouth–Waterloo near Fleet on 14 February 1967. With steam to spare, she makes light work of the four-coach semi-fast train on a crisp Winter's morning. *GPC*

On 10 June 1967, Winchfield provided the location for the best of about half a dozen passing train shots I achieved from 1964-7. Having the advantage of several miles of straight track, I became aware of two likely conflicting fast workings where I would have to be quick to gain a photo of each working. Fortunately, I had removed the telephoto lens I had been experimenting with for the standard lens and soon became aware the picture opportunity was going to be very tight. In the end the tripod was ideally positioned and I managed to capture 'WC' 34004 *Yeovil* on the 08.46 Bournemouth–Waterloo train meeting 'MN' 35030 *Elder Dempster Lines* on the 10.24SO Waterloo–Bournemouth service. With a closing speed of c150mph, this was a pretty unique photo opportunity. From a personal perspective, I was particularly pleased that Cecil J. Allen chose these photos to illustrate his article on the final Bulleid workings in September 1967 *Railway World. GPC*

Perhaps no picture illustrates the passing of the old regime quite as effectively as this. It is the evening of 9 June 1967, the last rostered date for steam traction on this working, and 'WC' 34013 *Okehampton* accelerates the 17.09 Waterloo–Salisbury commuter train from Winchfield station whilst new 4REP unit 3009 plus 8TC set forming the 1730 Waterloo–Bournemouth service seemingly passes the heavily loaded local. In fact 34013 was drawing away from the checked electric service which fortunately gave an opportunity to get a rear shot too with a swift change to a colour camera. *GPC both*

Rebuilt 'BB' 34089 *602 Squadron* barely disturbs the countryside as she approaches Hook with the 17.09 Waterloo–Salisbury commuter service on 26 May 1967. No 34089 was the last loco to be outshopped by Eastleigh the previous October. *GPC*

Just occasionally one of the Standard Class 4 4-6-0s would be given the opportunity to work a fast train on the main line. No 75074 was almost certainly deputising for more normal Bulleid or Standard 5 motive power but such workings in the last few weeks were not one-offs. Here the evening sun reflects on 75074 as she pounds on the up fast track working the 18.38 Salisbury–Waterloo (16.04 ex Exeter) on 29 May 1967. Introduced in 1955, and fitted with a double blastpipe after 1957 to the rather more elegant Brighton pattern (rather than the Swindon one), the locomotive with its high sided BR1B tender was a Southern engine for all its 11-year life, latterly based at Eastleigh. *GPC*

Back in Winchfield cutting on 3 June 1967, there is much anticipation for the imminent run of preserved 'A4' 4498 on its special working to Bournemouth. Yet again a 'local' train made for the better photo opportunity. With the benefit of the telephoto lens, I manage to achieve slight compression to give an overall more powerful feel to 'MN' 35023 *Holland-Afrika Line* as she pounds her mixed livery stock in the warming early Summer sun along the greyhound stretch to Basingstoke. Here at the head of the 09.24 Waterloo–Weymouth Saturday service, 35023 along with sister loco 35030 was to play a pivotal role in the last weekend of steam operation with the former having a reputation for free running. It was this engine that Bert Hooker famously took on his final run on a non-stop Waterloo–Salisbury on 15 November 1966 that achieved a 102mph maximum. *GPC*

A slightly earlier shot at Basingstoke but it shows what is thought to be one of the last Basingstoke–Salisbury local trains worked by a Class S15 on 16 September 1964. As we have seen earlier, the Moguls and 'S15s' managed to haul these services regularly until the end of the year and here Class S15 30839 stands at the platform having just reversed onto its rolling stock. *KGV*

An immaculate rebuilt 'Merchant Navy' No 35014 *Nederland Line* stands at the head of the now diverted 'Pines Express' with a complete rake of BR Mk1 maroon stock at Basingstoke on 5 September 1964. The story of BR management's diversion of this train in September 1962 from the more direct Somerset & Dorset route to help facilitate closure of that line is well known. The 'Pines', which operated between Manchester and Bournemouth, simply formed one further inter-regional service which would traverse the metals of all four English regions. No 35014 was delivered as part of the second batch of 'Merchant Navys' in 1945 and survived until March 1967 with a total of nearly 1.1 million miles. *KGV*

'BB' 34060 *25 Squadron* drifts into Basingstoke station with an afternoon Waterloo–Bournemouth service in September 1965. No 34060 was an Eastleigh loco that was withdrawn in June 1967, just over 20 years after introduction. A Standard Class 5 waits in the siding by the signal box with a rake of coaches, possibly for a local service to the south. *KGV*

An up Bournemouth–York/Newcastle service is here headed by Stanier Black 5 No 45198 in the Winter of 1965. For some reason it appears we have the driver on watering duties and an inspector present for the footplate trip. Next stop will be Oxford as the train will take Reading West Junction curve and the avoiding line at Didcot. Unusually 45198 was allocated to Croes Newydd shed but was a regular performer on this service for a while (she was sighted at Banbury on this service on 1 January 1966). She was ultimately reallocated to Wigan Springs Branch, from where she was withdrawn in September 1967. *KGV*

Ex GWR locomotives were frequent visitors to the SR main line south of Basingstoke. Here modified 'Hall' class 4-6-0 No 6998 *Burton Agnes Hall* comes off the Reading–Basingstoke line with a through York–Bournemouth train in September 1965. Built in BR days in 1949, 6998 was an Oxford loco and destined to be the last WR locomotive to be used on a passenger service (Oxford to Banbury) on 3 January 1966, after which she was withdrawn and privately purchased. *KGV*

Opposite: Rebuilt 'WC' 34018 *Axminster* restarts the down 'Pines Express' from Basingstoke on a cold day in December 1965. Though she had a reputation for fine running, 34018 is perhaps showing signs of a slightly uncared for existence with 'burning' around the bottom of the smokebox door. No 34018 was an Eastleigh loco at this date and survived until July 1967. *KGV*

Basingstoke shed was situated just to the west of the station. Here in September 1964, 'WC' 34048 *Crediton* is prominent with steam to spare with an unidentified WR 'Hall' class 4-6-0 behind. Alongside is Feltham-shedded 'S15' class 4-6-0 No 30823 with only two months to survive before withdrawal. No 34048 would survive until March 1966. *KGV*

Below: At Worting Junction the Exeter main line via Salisbury dives under Battledown flyover whilst the up main line from Southampton traverses the girder bridge. Initially the two lines crossed each other on the flat but as traffic increased, some relief was required. The flyover was opened in May 1897, enabling the up and down Salisbury lines to pass in tandem underneath so that four main line tracks continued to Basingstoke, whilst the main line south to Southampton remains dual tracked, apart from a passing loop, until Shawford. Here 'MN' 35026 *Lamport & Holt Line* is at full pelt on the down 'Bournemouth Belle' on 31 May 1965. This was during a short golden era for the 'Belle' when it was accelerated to a two-hour timing, shaving 10 minutes from the previous timetable, for the brief period from 1963 to 1965. Introduced in 1948, 35026 was withdrawn from Weymouth shed in March 1967 having run 858,874 miles. *RNT*

We deviate briefly down the Salisbury route. Steam working beyond Salisbury to Exeter had ceased at the start of the period under review but Salisbury continued to provide motive power for peak and relief services. Original 'BB' Pacific 34066 *Spitfire*, in grubby though complete condition, is approaching Salisbury station past the West box and the closed Market House branch that served the town centre until 1964. The picture was possibly taken on the same day and of the same working when photographed at Waterloo at the front of this section – perhaps photographer Ken Vernon had caught the fast 'Warship' service to arrive in time to capture the arrival of 34066. *KGV*

An interesting view of rebuilt 'BB' 34052 *Lord Dowding* at Salisbury in Autumn 1966. Almost certainly on an enthusiasts special (probably the SCTS run of 4 October 1966 that went onto Ludgershall behind 'MN' 35023) the photo shows the lines leading out to the west from the station along with the magnificent Salisbury West box. A few cable wagons are parked to the side of the station. *KGV*

We are at Salisbury where 'MN' 35022 *Holland-America Line* has arrived for water and a crew change before taking its 'Exeter Flyer' tour forward on 12 September 1965. The traincrew are having an informal chat after watering the engine whilst the fireman is high in the tender pushing the coal forward for the remaining journey. To enable rapid turnround times it was common at Salisbury for a local man to undertake the coal pushing whilst the fireman attended to the watering. With an exchange between driver and fireman, 35022 receives some final valve gear lubrication before resuming her trip west. Looking as magnificent as she does, it seems ironic that 35022 was withdrawn from Weymouth shed just a few months later in May 1966 (18 years old, and 10 years after rebuilding) and was originally the first choice loco for the Merchant Navy Loco Preservation Society. *KGV*

Inside Salisbury shed BR Standard Class 4 2-6-0 No 76007 looks in fine condition, though not in steam, on 18 March 1967. Built in 1953 and allocated to Salisbury from 1958, 76007 was to survive until the end and was operational in the last week. *GPC*

No 34006 *Bude* looks to be under repair with the cylinder cover removed. We saw earlier 34006 being overhauled in Eastleigh in 1966 but this looks to be a repair too far on 18 March 1967. Records show that she was withdrawn the following day after an illustrious career that included the interchange trials of 1948 along with sister locos 34004 and 34005. No 34006 worked the Plymouth–Bristol and Marylebone–Manchester routes. *GPC*

Eastleigh Works loco card for 34006 confirming withdrawal the following day, 19 March 1967. *GPC*

'WC' 34034 *Honiton* heads an inter-regional Bournemouth–York working on a Summer's day in 1966 and approaches Shawford Junction signal box on the southern approaches to Winchester. The train formation is interesting as it includes a pre-war Gresley teak brake end that has been liveried in BR(E) maroon. Some of these vehicles survived into BR corporate blue/grey into the 1970s. The track formation from the Didcot, Newbury & Southampton (DN&S) line is still in place as, having opened in 1885 and lost its passenger service in 1960, it was being used as a freight route until August 1966. I can recall pacing trains past the Hockley Viaduct whilst in a car on the Winchester by-pass in the early 1960s. The viaduct has been preserved and is now a footpath/cycleway. The original alignment and a newly ballasted relief line are visible. *RH*

With electrification and closure of the through DN&S route, looking south west, the junction has been removed and the track re-aligned for the Shawford relief line. Here, with exactly two months of steam working left, 'WC' 34023 *Blackmore Vale* hauls the 09.20 Waterloo–Southampton Docks boat train, the 'Iberia', on 9 May 1967. No 34023 survived to the end and used sparingly possibly because she had fortunately become an early target of the preservationists. *GPC*

Above: Eastleigh station provides the venue for the next few photos, all taken in September 1964. Here 'WC' 34101 *Hartland* is hauling a down boat train to Southampton. There is no sign of forthcoming electrification, with the only concession to modernity being the AWS (Automatic Warning System) ramp on the up fast track. *KGV*

The down 'Bournemouth Belle' pounds through Eastleigh behind 'BB' 34085 *501 Squadron*. The fine signal box can be seen in the background as 34085 hustles its full rake past. *KGV*

… to retun three hours later with the same locomotive and train formation on the up working. The carriage sidings at the head of the carriage works can be seen to the left whilst part of the locomotive works building can be seen in the middle background. No 34085 was withdrawn a year later in September 1965, just five years after having been rebuilt and having only achieved a lifetime mileage of 661,415. *KGV*

Some two years later on 17 September 1966 the third rail is in situ whilst Standard Class 5 73022 pauses at Eastleigh station on a three-coach local train, probably the 14.10 all stations Eastleigh to Bournemouth. A Nine Elms locomotive, 73022 was withdrawn in April 1967. *KGV*

An unusual picture in terms of motive power and location, taken on 17 September 1966. Two Standard Class 4 tanks, 80016 and 80152, are working an Eastleigh–Salisbury–Eastleigh leg of an enthusiasts' train that started the day from Victoria behind 4472 *Flying Scotsman* travelling via Brighton to Eastleigh. They are shown paused at Dean as a Hampshire unit approaches on a Salisbury bound train. *KGV*

Fourteen 'USA' tanks were bought by the Southern Railway after World War 2, mainly for work around Southampton Docks, where they replaced more diminutive classes like the 'B4' 0-4-0 tanks. The latter were estimated to require boiler repairs costing over £1,500 each that would take up to 18 months to complete so after trials at Southampton docks, the SR tendered £2,500 per unit for 14 of the 46 'USAs' being stored at Newbury Racecourse. Some 382 of these powerful Baldwin tanks were built and distributed over Europe and the Middle East. The SR locos survived at the docks until 1962 and then received a new lease of life in shunting roles around the SR. Some received a new coat of Southern Railway green paint whilst retaining their BR numbers as in this picture of 30073 running outside Eastleigh Works' main building in January 1966. Others were withdrawn from main service but awarded DS numbers and names as departmental locomotives that could be seen mainly at Eastleigh and Ashford. No 30073 was withdrawn July 1967. *KGV*

Below: Standard Class 4 75077, still replete with its Ron Cover replacement numberplate, is leaving her home depot of Eastleigh with the Cowans breakdown crane on 17 June 1967 to attend some incident up the line. Having reached this stage, 75077 was to survive until the last day of steam – a life of 12 years. *GPC*

BR Standard Class 5 73115 *King Pellinore*, a Guildford engine, is fully coaled in light steam and ready to go in Eastleigh shed on 23 July 1966. No 73115 was withdrawn in March 1967, having first been allocated to Nine Elms in November 1955. Already shorn of nameplates, these Standard 5s continuing in the 'King Arthur' series barely carried their plates for five years. *GPC*

It's literally a steaming hot day on 23 July 1966 and Eastleigh shed is showing signs of being rundown even though it has another year to service surviving steam locos. The 'USAs' were part of the busy scene and here class member No 30069 stands on the ashpit road awaiting her next duty. She survived until the end in July 1967. *GPC*

'WC' 34037 *Clovelly* is being prepared for her next run on 17 June 1967. She is clearly devoid of nameplates as there are only three weeks to go until withdrawal but the fireman is busying himself breaking up coal in the tender which probably makes a welcome change from dealing with much low-grade coal and 'nutty slack'. Eastleigh benefited in its final days from the transfer of the Salisbury foreman, Claud Dare, who brought his cleanliness standards to the Eastleigh fleet. He was willing to sanction weekend overtime to give the remaining locos a more burnished finish. No 34037 entered service in July 1946, was rebuilt in 1958 and completed 810,658 miles in service. *GPC*

An unidentified Standard Class 4 2-6-0 equipped with double blastpipe and BR1B tender heads a local service from Bournemouth around the tight Northam curve outside Southampton in May 1965. The check rail can be seen on both tracks which also helped add to the distinct grating noise as trains negotiated the curve. The severity of the curve was quoted as a reason why the surplus 'Duchess' Pacifics from the LMR could not be operated on the Bournemouth route. The spring lighting helps capture the upper quadrant semaphore signals along with period beer advertising. *RH*

'MN' 35027 *Port Line* rounds the curve at Tunnel Junction with a Waterloo-bound train just outside Southampton, past what looks like an old bombsite to one side and the magnificent tall old LSWR signal box in this photograph taken in 1965. *RH*

Standard Class 4 4-6-0 No 75075 has stopped at St Denys with an Eastleigh–Bournemouth local service some time in 1966. An Eastleigh loco, she too survived until the end of steam. Remarkably 75075 found its way to Nine Elms from Weymouth on 7 and 8 July, where she was maintained in steam on the last day, it being speculated for any potential working of the breakdown train. No 75075 entered traffic in November 1955 and was allocated to Eastleigh for the last four years of its life. *RH*

The smaller Standard Class 4 2-6-0s were introduced in 1953 to a Doncaster design. Some 115 were built and found service all over the country. The SR had 42 examples with the larger BR1B tenders. Here 76067, a Bournemouth loco, is seen near Netley on the Fareham–St Denys line with an evening parcels train to Salisbury in the Summer of 1965. *RH*

It is Sunday 19 September 1965 and the engineers have possession of the main line. Rather than be diverted over the 'Alps', 'WC' 34012 *Launceston* has been diverted via the Portsmouth direct route and is here passing Peasemarsh Junction on her way to regain the main line at Southampton. No 34012 looks in fine condition with a full set of plates but would be withdrawn just over a year later in December 1966. *RNT*

Stanier Black 5 44942 4-6-0 emerges from the tunnel at Southampton with a York–Bournemouth service on 28 March 1966. A Banbury allocated locomotive from October 1965 to September 1966, 44942 would undertake a range of duties on the inter-regional trains and also on the last workings of the Great Central (GC) line to Marylebone. She returned north to Shrewsbury and Lostock Hall after the closure of ex GC main line in September 1966 but did survive until June 1968 in consequence. It has been estimated that up to 35 Black 5s worked the route during 1966 in addition to Class 9F 92002. *KGV*

At the northern end of the station, 'BB' 34064 *Fighter Command* also receives the attention of the young fireman at the head of its Waterloo-bound train in Autumn 1965. No 34064 was fitted with Dr Giesl's patented ejector in 1962. The narrow, elongated exhaust provided fuel efficiency and increased power that allegedly gave the 'Battle of Britain' the performance of the larger 'Merchant Navy' Pacific. At a unit cost of c£700 (£14,000 in 2017 values), the modification was deemed too late to warrant being fitted to the 20 other members of the class as was originally planned. However, preserved sister engine 34092 *City of Wells* has been retro-fitted with the system. Also it was reported that Dr Giesl himself was nearly a casualty during the testing of 34064 when he stepped in front of a passing train but managed to clear the line just in time. No 34064 was the 1,000th engine constructed at Brighton, having been completed in July 1947, and ran a total of 759,666 miles before withdrawal in May 1966 following an uncontrolled slip near Basingstoke, where the loco was stored for some while. *KGV*

Below: Class 4 Standard 2-6-0 76026 had earlier run to Southampton with a football excursion from Bournemouth. This is believed to be the return working after the Saints had suffered a defeat to visitors Sheffield Wednesday on 1 October 1966. Nevertheless, some fine Autumn sunshine serves to illuminate train and signal gantry to good effect at the southern end of the station. A fortnight later, on 15 October 1966, 76026 headed one of the last steam workings over the S&D route, closed in March, as far as Blandford Forum with a LCGB railtour. *GPC*

It is New Year's Eve 1966 at Southampton as Class 4 Standard tank 80139 waits to start the 18.30 Southampton–Bournemouth local. These local services would continue to be mainly steam worked for the duration of steam up to July 1967 and 80139 would itself be retired at the same time, some 11 years after being built. *GPC*

Opposite left: BR Standard Class 4 tank 80152 leaves Southampton with the Civic Centre bell tower prominent in the background working the 16.28 Bournemouth–Eastleigh local train on 7 May 1967. Even at this late stage, the local workings remained largely steam worked with some spirited stop/starts achieved on relatively lightly loaded trains. *GPC*

Right: 'WC' 34008 *Padstow* takes water at Southampton on 8 April 1967 and has the 'all away' to head her inter-regional train, the 10.30 Poole to York. Unfortunately history does not record whether or how far into WR territory she worked but she hauled the balancing working, the 08.30 Newcastle to Bournemouth, back the same day. Steam was supposed to be supplanted by diesel motive power on these trains from the previous month but substitutions remained frequent to the end. *GPC*

On New Year's Eve 1966 rebuilt 'WC' 34032 *Camelford* glistens in the afternoon sun at Southampton at the head of the 12.59 Bournemouth–Waterloo service. This might be regarded as a run of the mill shot but it is significant because 34032 was one of three Bulleids (the others being 34026 and 34005) and seven Standards reinstated to traffic at Eastleigh and returned to steam that December to handle the extra Christmas traffic. It is not clear when they were finally withdrawn, as the official date recorded for 34032 was 8 October 1966 but it is unlikely they lasted more than a week or two into 1967. The previous year 34032 worked the 13.00 Waterloo to Exeter on 29 November 1965, this being the last timetabled passenger service to be worked by steam. *GPC*

The works loco card for No 34032 showing its premature withdrawal date. *GPC*

From 5 March 1967, the diagrams for the inter-regional services were recast and signalled the end of through steam working. For the last through York working, rebuilt 'WC' 34004 *Yeovil*, complete with all plates and something of a rarity at this stage, had been turned out in fine condition to work the morning and balancing evening return service. As luck would have it, there was just enough light around in the winter setting sun at Southampton for 1/30th sec F2 exposure. The dock cranes are visible in the distance as 34004 waits to depart with safety valves lifting. It's interesting to note that steam continued to make incursions into WR territory with 35030 reported at Reading on 29 April 1967 covering for a failed diesel to work the southbound portion of a Newcastle–Bournemouth service. *GPC*

One of the many times in 1967 that a shortage of Type 4 diesel power resulted in steam substitution on the 'Bournemouth Belle.' 'WC' 34013 *Okehampton* threads the Totton Causeway, where the River Test flows into Southampton Water, on 25 February 1967. By now the rake has lost its Pullman brake ends but at least the first vehicle is in SR green though the last is in the new corporate blue/grey that does not exactly co-ordinate with the brown/cream Pullman livery. *GPC*

No 35030 *Elder Dempster Lines* is impressively clean as she accelerates a Waterloo–Bournemouth train past Millbrook in February 1966. No 35030 was to be active until the end of steam, hauling the very last up steam working on 9 July 1967. *KGV*

Opposite: A grimy 'BB' 34060 *25 Squadron* heads the 10.40 Plymouth–Brighton past Millbrook on the approaches to Southampton on 28 March 1966. Steam was reinstated on this cross country service in January 1966 until the end of April that year to provide steam heating for these long-distance passenger services. *KGV*

The Fawley branch from the main line at Totton on the south side of Southampton Water, opened in 1926, was clearly important for the burgeoning Esso oil terminal. Although much traffic is carried via pipeline (the direct link to Heathrow being carried in pipes buried in the main line earthworks for part of the way) there were still regular tanker workings that traversed the branch. The passenger service was lost in February 1966 and the line only finally closed in 2016. Nevertheless, it received a number of steam specials and here a charming combination of 'USA' tank 0-6-0s work a LCGB tour on 9 April 1967. No 30064 is resplendent in her later Southern green livery whilst No 30069 wears her mid-1950s black livery as she still sports the older BR 'cycling lion' decal that was superseded from 1956. *KGV*

On a beautiful Spring day, 4 March 1967, New Forest ponies laze and graze nonchalantly as Class 4 Standard 76026 accelerates the 12.56 Southampton–Bournemouth service away from Brockenhurst. Built in 1953 and allocated to the SR all its life, it was latterly a Bournemouth engine and survived until July 1967. *GPC*

On 1 April 1967 Standard Class 4 tank 80152 stands at Brockenhurst station at the head of a Lymington branch train on the last weekend of steam working, which she shared with Ivatt tank No 41312. Diesel units were introduced from 3 April 1967 to work the 5.6-mile route to the ferry terminal serving Freshwater on the Isle of Wight. The line was subsequently electrified in July 1967 and survives today. This locomotive was operational on the last weekend of steam when it worked a two-coach portion of the 08.35 Waterloo–Bournemouth from Southampton Central to the Eastern Docks. *GPC*

On 4 March 1967, as I walked back along the road from the open country of the New Forest, I heard the whistle of a Bulleid Pacific down the track. I quickly crossed some scrubland to find the lineside, looking straight down to Brockenhurst station. There was then a volcanic start with heavy slipping as 'MN' 35008 *Orient Line* got to grips with her load. The smoke was black and vertical but I was too far away to record it. By the time 35008 reached me, she had regained her 'legs' at the head of the 13.30 Waterloo–Bournemouth and was rapidly gaining speed. No 35008 was always recognisable in 1967, even when de-plated, because at some stage she had received a 'ding' on the smokebox door that caused the depression immediately behind the dart. *GPC*

Standard 4 80011 works the 15.00 Brockenhurst–Lymington service on 4 March 1967, just one month before steam was eliminated. The train makes an atmospheric picture, having just left the main line, which is visible in the background, as 80011, built at Brighton in 1951, trundles towards Lymington. A Bournemouth-allocated loco, she was not withdrawn until July 1967. *GPC*

This is the one that almost got away. The date is 20 August 1966 and the working is much referred to in the contemporary railway press and in subsequent books though photographic evidence is scant. Fortunately Roger Holmes was on the lineside in the New Forest to capture this rare scene of a '9F' 2-10-0 working one of the inter-regional Bournemouth–York expresses. The loco probably worked a freight into the region and was being returned to home territory, thus avoiding light engine working. The precise location is not identified but Roger has succeeded in capturing the '9F' at speed, showing its ten coupled 5ft driving wheels to good effect. No 92002 was one of the first batch of '9Fs' built in January 1954 and was subsequently fitted with a double chimney. At the time of this working 92002 was allocated to Tyseley and worked this train through to Banbury and reportedly kept good time. She was eventually withdrawn from Birkenhead in November 1967. *RH*

Original, Giesl-fitted, Pacific 'BB' 34064 *Fighter Command* is shown between Sway and Brockenhurst in this panned view towards the end of her life, in April 1966. *RNT*

A view of Bournemouth shed when hosting newly preserved guest visitor 'A4' class Pacific No 4498 *Sir Nigel Gresley* that worked a weekend of specials on 3 and 4 June 1967. Ken Vernon has travelled behind his beloved 'A4' and also captured on shed Bulleid Pacific 34023 *Blackmore Vale* and Standard Class 4 2-6-0 No 76009. We shall return to both the shed and the visiting 'A4' later. *KGV*

No 34023 *Blackmore Vale* has just worked the down 10.24 SO Waterloo–Weymouth train into Bournemouth station on 3 June 1967. This is the same train depicted in the introduction (see page 7). She probably came off at this stage for servicing at the depot as she was diagrammed to work the Southampton–Salisbury leg of the 'A4' special later in the day. It is not known if she worked light engine to Southampton or was used on a local service. *KGV*

Above: 'BB' 34051 *Winston Churchill* stands at Bournemouth West on 2 May 1965 just before heading the return 'Wessex Downsman' to Waterloo. As we have seen earlier, she was famous for working the Churchill funeral train on 29 January 1965 and consequently earned her place on the preservation list. *KGV*

The works card shows that 34051 was in works for a Light Casual for two months from October to December 1964, thus ensuring she was in good condition for her special duties in January 1965 and obviating the use of reserve engine 34064. *GPC*

On 7 May 1967 the LCGB ran its last special 'Dorset Coast Express', which would make two runs down the Swanage branch which had been dieselised in September 1966. Here 'WC' 34023 *Blackmore Vale* pauses at Wareham before heading to Worgret Junction to make the 10-mile trip to Swanage over the line that opened in 1885 and for which BR, in a late piece of Beeching implementation, posted a closure notice to take effect from September 1968. Alternative services were found to be inadequate and ultimately the line did not close until January 1972. *KGV*

In a scene that has hardly changed in 50 years, 34023 *Blackmore Vale* attracts a crowd of admiring enthusiasts having arrived at the Swanage terminus on 7 May 1967 on one of its two trips that day. *KGV*

Two pristine Ivatt 2-6-2 tanks, Nos 41301 and 41284, stand at Swanage ready to take their train back to Wareham before going on to tackle the Bridport branch on 27 February 1966. The scene is little changed apart from the replacement of the original Swanage signal box on the right (southern) side to left (northern) side in preservation days. Both 41301 and 41284 were Weymouth-allocated locomotives at the time though 41301 was withdrawn in September 1966 whilst 41284 was transferred to Nine Elms to survive until March 1967. *KGV*

BR Standard Class 4 No 76013, allocated to Bournemouth shed, simmers at the Swanage branch terminus waiting to depart with an afternoon service train to Wareham in Summer 1966. *KGV*

In the Summer of 1966, rebuilt Bulleid Pacific 'BB' 34088 *213 Squadron* sweeps a Waterloo–Weymouth train through the Bincombe Tunnels as she approaches Wishing Well Halt on the 1 in 50 downgrade towards Weymouth. At this time 34088 was an Eastleigh-allocated locomotive which was withdrawn in March 1967 having run a mere 656, 583 miles in slightly over 18 years. *RH*

Below: On 3 September 1966 rebuilt 'WC' 34001 *Exeter* is at the head of a Waterloo-bound train that is banked by no less than 'MN' 35029 *Ellerman Lines* to assist on this 12-coach train on the Upwey gradient. No 34001 was withdrawn in July 1967 but 35029 went out in style just three days after this photo was taken. John Corkhill (he of painted numberplate fame) was riding the 17.30 Weymouth–Waterloo behind 35029. She whipped through Winchester at 75mph and crested Roundwood summit at 85mph. She took to the greyhound stretch and reached 104mph at Hook before being checked by signals from which she again recovered to hit 96mph at Farnborough. However it all came to a sticky end near Woking when a superheater flue gave way. The train was brought to a halt and had to be diesel-hauled into Waterloo. But what a way to go – especially as 35029 survives as the famously sectioned locomotive at the National Railway Museum in York. *RNT*

Upwey bank on the climb out of Weymouth is the steepest grade on the Southern Region network. It is 4 miles of 1 in 74 and 1 in 50 and often necessitated a banker or double-heading to get heavy trains up the grade, especially as they were climbing after a mere 1.5 miles of level track. Two Standards start the gruelling climb with a heavy passenger working. Standard 4 2-6-0 76008 double-heads Standard 5 4-6-0 73087 on 3 September 1966. The slightly more burnished 76008 is a Salisbury-allocated loco whereas 73087 was a Guildford loco. No 73087 was built in 1955, named *Linette* and spent most of its life on the Somerset & Dorset route. She was withdrawn a month after this photo was taken. *RNT*

Earlier in the day Standard Class 5 73083 *Pendragon*, a Weymouth-allocated loco, approaches Upwey with a Waterloo-bound train on the climb out of Weymouth, with assistance provided by Standard Class 4 76008. No 73083 would be withdrawn later in the same month. *RNT*

Ivatt tank 41301 has reached Weymouth on railtour duty on 27 February 1966 and is being replenished with water in preparation for the trip to Bridport and Yeovil Junction, for which it and sister loco 41284 topped and tailed the train for the Bridport branch. *KGV*

Salisbury-allocated 'BB' 34089 *602 Squadron*, maintained in burnished condition, is being turned at Weymouth MPD on 18 June 1967. Many books have been written on the merits/demerits of the original and rebuilt Bulleid Pacifics but no one can doubt the elegance of either machine, the rebuilds dating from 1956 with their Walschaerts valve gear and other key changes. Such were the running and repair costs of the 'Merchant Navy' class, consideration was even given to scrapping them and replacing them with Standard 'Britannia' Pacifics – the 'Britannias' had running costs at only 60% of the 'MNs'. Even the arguably more complicated Gresley 'A4s' had servicing costs significantly lower than Bulleid's finest. The original 1955 financial justification for rebuilding all Bulleid's Pacifics was based on a further 20-year life to 1975 with a conversion cost of £5,615 per locomotive – equivalent to £133,000 today. The lifetime net savings for the 140-locomotive fleet were estimated at £2.05 million in 1954, a value equivalent to over £40 million today. Even with a truncated life, the lower operating, repair costs and increased availability made conversion viable against the 1953 cost of a new 'Britannia' of £25,330. Either way, even though Bulleid did not approve of the conversion work, enthusiasts gained as, with the programme cut short in 1961, we got to experience both versions of this fine locomotive design. *KGV*

The date 18 June 1967 saw the last privately sponsored railtour (by the RCTS) on the SR and involved a total of four Bulleids plus a green Standard Class 5 4-6-0. Here the train departs Weymouth for the climb of Upwey Bank behind original 'WC' 34023 *Blackmore Vale* and rebuilt 'WC' 34108 *Wincanton*. The latter locomotive was built in April 1950 and withdrawn in the week following this special, thereby failing to reach the end of steam by three weeks. *KGV*

Rebuilt 'MN' 35028 *Clan Line* makes a fine portrait standing at Weymouth in 1966. *KGV*

'WC' 34023 *Blackmore Vale* was much in use in the last few months of steam on the SR. She was taking part in railtour activities on 18 June 1967 and can be seen being serviced at Weymouth MPD before double-heading the return leg of the tour. *KGV*

Standard Class 4 76026 and Standard 5 73029 prepare to depart Weymouth for Bournemouth on 7 May 1967 with the return of the 'Dorset Coast Express'. Both locomotives survived to the end of steam but 73029 had a rather more varied career. Delivered new to Blackpool in 1951, she had been transferred to Swindon by 1957 via Bristol and Carmarthen. Then a transfer to Weymouth meant the rest of 73029's existence was on the Southern with Nine Elms being her last shed allocation. *KGV*

The superb lines of the Bulleid rebuilds is shown to great effect in this picture of 35028 *Clan Line* at Weymouth station where the wintry afternoon sun provides ideal lighting conditions on 27 February 1966. No 35028 was reported to have performed effortlessly on the 'Dorset Belle' tour. She was a favourite amongst the crews, along with 35022 and 35023, and, of course, was to be privately preserved and remains running today. *KGV*

Foreigners Come South

The year 1966 was characterised by the visits of several 'foreign' locomotives such as an 'A4', 'A3' and 'V2', and a further 'Last Steam to Exeter' special behind Peppercorn 'A2' Pacific *Blue Peter*. At one stage a brace of 'Jubilees' was planned but unfortunately was too difficult to organise – though getting light locomotives from Scotland can't have been easy as borne out by the multiple failure of the 'V2' when it did finally arrive. Additionally, Stanier 'Black 5s' and the occasional 'Britannia' (70002 and 70014) made it onto service trains that Summer.

'A4' 60024 *Kingfisher* made it down from Scotland for a weekend of special workings in March 1966. Bert Hooker records in his book how he was a tad disappointed not to drive this fine loco having been entrusted with the immaculate *Mallard* some three years earlier on a similar trip celebrating the 15th anniversary of the locomotive exchanges. Class V2 60919 was booked for a Weymouth special but never got anywhere near hauling her allotted train. Despite chasing it light engine to Eastleigh, hot boxes meant that original 'WC' 34002 *Salisbury* was in charge for the Waterloo–Southampton and return legs. No 60532 *Blue Peter* had an eventful trip to Exeter in August 1966, being forced to a halt for a blow-up on Honiton Bank. 'Britannia' 70004 *William Shakespeare* took over for the rest of the tour but was running 90min late on the return. Nevertheless 70004 found herself at the head of the 17.23 'Ocean Liner' Waterloo–Southampton Docks train on 16 August. The 'A3' special was of course *Flying Scotsman* on the 'Farnborough Flyer' excursion for the Farnborough Air Show in September 1966 and went onto Brighton line specials the following day.

A few 'A4s' survivied to the end of Summer 1966 having been transferred to Scotland following dieselisation of the East Coast Main Line in 1963. The LCGB had the imagination to request 60024 *Kingfisher* for a weekend of steam workings to Weymouth and Exeter over the weekend of 26/27 March 1966. Finally this section includes visits by 'K4' The *Great Marquess, 9f Evening Star* and the 'local' foreigner Austerity *Gordon* from the Longmoor Military Railway.

'A4' 60024 *Kingfisher* is shown at Yeovil Junction on the Exeter trip with Driver Hackett, having taken over from Driver Porter of Nine Elms, awaiting the 'rightaway' from the signalman. *KGV*

60024 *Kingfisher* is being serviced at Exmouth Junction shed having arrived on the 27 March 1966 special. Although steam services to Exeter were all but eliminated by the WR in September 1964, Exmouth Junction shed facilities were retained for a further two years which assisted enormously in running the numerous 'Last Steam to Exeter' specials in 1965/6. No 60024's return to Scotland was scheduled to make minimal use of light running by working the 10.30 Waterloo as far as Bournemouth and then run the northbound 'Pines Express' but a collapsed brick arch thwarted the plan. Built in December 1938 and fitted with the Kylchap double chimney in 1958, 60024 had a further six months in service and was withdrawn when steam ceased on the Aberdeen services in September 1966. Whilst the last timetabled train on 3 September 1966 was operated by sister loco 60019 *Bittern*, 60024 *Kingfisher* covered a failed diesel 10 days later and this was to be the last Aberdeen–Glasgow steam service. *KGV*

Sharing the passenger services with the 'A4s' between Aberdeen/Dundee and Glasgow were the three surviving Peppercorn 'A2' Pacifics in 1965/1966. However, by the Summer only 60530 *Sayajirao* and 60532 *Blue Peter* were left in service. Of the two, 60532 was in rather better condition, at least externally, and 60530, though not officially withdrawn until November 1966, was taken out of service at the end of August. So, the LCGB once again got a Scottish loco to run south for an 'A2'-hauled Waterloo–Exeter special on 14 August 1966. This was at some risk to the Scottish services as the serviceable 'A4s' were reduced to two examples only at this stage. Here the 1948-built loco, equipped with multiple valve regulator, waits at Waterloo for departure with the Shell-Mex building towering above in the background. *KGV*

On another of those brilliant Summer 1966 days, 60532 *Blue Peter* makes light work of the load of SR Mk1 and Bulleid stock as she hauls the 'A2 Commemorative' special through Deepcut on 14 August 1966. Her performance was lacklustre to say the least and she was soon in trouble with poor steaming, as evidenced here with a cylinder cock jammed open for the whole trip. *GPC*

Peppercorn A2 60532 *Blue Peter* pauses at Axminster. By the time she reached Exeter she was two hours late with reports of needing a 'blow up' on Honiton Bank to raise more steam. The plan was to run the return trip up the WR main line to Westbury and then for 'Britannia' 70004 to take the train to Salisbury where the 'A2', having been serviced, would continue to Waterloo. *Blue Peter* returned to Scotland and continued to run the Glasgow–Aberdeen route plus a memorable steam trip over the Waverley in the Autumn. She was withdrawn at the end of 1966 and was to languish at Thornton Junction shed in Fife where she could be seen in 1968 as funds were raised, helped by the eponymous BBC programme, before restoration took place under the watchful eye of Geoffrey Drury at the ICI Wilton complex in the 1970s. *KGV*

No 70004 *William Shakespeare* had been one of the SR-allocated locos in the mid 1950s working the 'Golden Arrow' service from Victoria. For the 14 August 1966 LCGB trip the locomotive had been brought south from Stockport Edgeley for ostensibly the section from Westbury to Salisbury only. Since *Blue Peter* was three hours late by Westbury, the 'Britannia' took the train all the way to Waterloo and arrived only 80 minutes late. I recall waiting at the lineside for over an hour and giving up the wait as even for Summer it was getting too dark to get an action shot. Tenaciously, the SR retained the loco for a few days and it worked a boat train and a commuter service. No 70004 was withdrawn at the end of 1967. *KGV*

SIR NIGEL GRESLEY

No 4498 is being turned on the turntable at Bournemouth on 3 June 1967 whilst being prepared for her return trip to Waterloo. Over the weekend speeds of 90mph were recorded for this immaculately maintained loco. *KGV*

A contrasting scene at Waterloo on 3 June 1967 where preserved Gresley 'A4' Pacific 4498 *Sir Nigel Gresley* in immaculately preserved garter blue livery stands alongside a filthy and unidentifiable BR Standard 4 tank. Formerly BR No 60007, the A4 Preservation Society had been busy raising the £3,000 to buy the locomotive. Withdrawn from Aberdeen Ferryhill in February 1966, *Sir Nigel* was bought by the preservation group in May. She was taken to Crewe for light restoration and repaint. Sister locomotive 60026 *Miles Beevor* was despatched south from Scotland to Crewe in August 1966 to provide some much needed spare parts. No 4498 emerged from Crewe in early 1967 and was used extensively on the BR network. *KGV*

Here you should note the disparity between the locomotive headboard and the loco in use. Between the 'A4' and 'A2' trips, the LCGB again tried an ambitious tour by bringing a Gresley 'V2' 2-6-2 south from Dundee Tay Bridge shed to run a Waterloo–Exeter tour. Whilst at the time there were at least three serviceable 'V2s', they were unlucky to get No 60919. It failed at Nine Elms shed and when that was fixed it ran south to Eastleigh where it failed again and was taken back to Basingstoke in the hope it might be attached to the last leg of the tour. It was not to be. 'WC' 34002 *Salisbury* had charge of the train the whole day and even managed some 90mph running. Here she is shown in full flight emerging from the cutting at Winchfield on 3 July 1966. In the end the last steam from Exeter was hauled by sister loco 34019 *Bideford* on 13 November 1966 having worked the down direction on the WR from Westbury to Exeter – almost a year after the WR steam ban had been implemented. *GPC*

More of a foreigner from the West, this is indeed an unusual picture. The last steam locomotive built by BR at Swindon in March 1960, No 92220 *Evening Star*, is heading a special over the 'Alps' on 20 September 1964. By this time she had been transferred from Bath Green Park to Cardiff East Dock (hence the occasional sighting on the 'Red Dragon' from Swansea to Paddington) and was working a Waterloo–Yeovil leg via a circuitous route that took in Aldershot, Alton, Ropley and rejoined the main line at Winchester Junction. Here *Evening Star* is climbing Medstead Bank. She would be withdrawn barely six months later, just five years old – evidence indeed of a flawed motive power development policy when a life of 25 years plus could have reasonably been expected! *RNT*

The privately preserved *Flying Scotsman* restored to LNER livery by Alan Pegler in 1963 is seen here at the head of the 'Farnborough Flyer' on 10 September 1966. The 'Flyer' was a regular event linked to the Farnborough Airshow at the Royal Aircraft Establishment. In latter years, the loco was often a preserved example of some type though in the 1950s the author recalls a double-headed 'T9' and Standard 5 on one occasion. Here 4472 has just rounded Pirbright Curve on the special from Doncaster organised under the auspices of the Gainsborough Model Railway Society and is catching the tail end of the 12.35 Waterloo–Bournemouth (with 'WC' 34023 at its head). Your author is actually on the footbridge in the background but my photo was only in black and white. *RNT*

So maybe here we are stretching the concept of foreigners from the north. The Longmoor Military Railway (LMR) War Department 2-10-0 was built at the Vulcan Works at Runcorn but spent its life on this military training line that formed a loop in the Hants/Surrey countryside between Bordon and Liss. Locos mainly comprised 'WDs' and 'J94' saddle tanks at this stage but this is a unique tour. No 600 *Gordon* sits at the head of an enthusiasts' train formed of SR green stock that ran on two occasions in April 1966. Two surviving Moguls operated the first leg to Woking but then on both dates No 600 ran down the main line from Woking to Guildford, Haslemere and Liss, where it joined the LMR network and subsequently took the train from Bordon to Staines. Whilst the LMR remained operational with steam until 1969, the 2-10-0s were never allowed onto the main line again – they picked up tour trains at Liss to run round the Hollywater Loop. After the army vacated the site, David Shepherd's locos had a brief incarnation at the Liss end of the system and he hoped to purchase/lease the rest. Local opposition ensured the line remained closed. *KGV*

Resplendent in its blue and red livery, No 600 *Gordon* sits outside Longmoor shed on 30 April 1966 between two 'J94' saddle tanks. Whilst the fleet were maintained by army personnel, the locomotives themselves were overhauled and repainted at Eastleigh. I can remember one works visit where some enthusiasts had absolutely no idea where the 2-10-0 was from, convinced the 'LMR' initials stood for London Midland Region. I didn't disabuse them! *KGV*

Built in 1938, the three-cylinder Gresley 2-6-0 'K4' class was built specifically for the Scottish lines such as the West Highland. Formerly BR No 61994, she was withdrawn in 1961 and saved by enthusiast Viscount Garnock who had the locomotive restored at Inverurie Works and repainted into her original LNER livery. The class only amounted to six examples and one of these Thompson insisted on converting to a two-cylinder class 'K1/1'. Here, on 12 March 1967, 3442 has ventured deep into the south and is standing at Victoria at the head of a special to Brighton which continued onto Chichester and Southampton before returning to Preston Park. The current owner John Cameron has announced the 'K4s' retirement to static exhibition in 2017. *KGV*

The Last Week – 2 to 9 July 1967

The last SR specials at premium prices were scheduled a week before the end of steam when both 35008 *Orient Line* and 35028 *Clan Line* had their nameplates restored and were 'bulled up' to look the part. No 35008 headed the 09.55 departure to Weymouth whilst 35028 hauled the 12.15 to Bournemouth. Both specials were well executed, with the Weymouth train recording a maximum of 90mph. Perhaps the highlight was the double-heading of 35007 and 35008 from Weymouth to Bournemouth on the return run.

Ahead of both trains 'WC' 34025 *Whimple* took out an excursion at a 'normal' fare as the 09.33 Waterloo–Bournemouth.

In the last week or so of operation there were several exceptional runs on the newly upgraded track on which the line limit was to be raised to 100mph for the new REP units. With the dying moments for steam, many enginemen were looking for their last fling, encouraged by the many enthusiasts filling the front coaches and corridors. No 35003 *Royal Mail* at the head of the 18.15 Weymouth–Waterloo on 26 June 1967 covered the 3.3 miles between Winchfield and Fleet in 1min 56sec at an average of 102.4mph and achieved a peak of 106mph through Fleet, admittedly with a load of only five vehicles or 170 tons. Ron Cover (*Steam World*, April 1982) personally recalls 96mph behind 35008 *Orient Line* and 93mph behind the rather worn unrebuilt 34102 *Lapford* (some others claimed 100mph at Bramshot Halt) and also mentions 35008 reaching 100mph at Andover (see later) and 35007 *Aberdeen Commonwealth* 97mph at Fleet, with 34095 *Brentnor* and 35028 *Clan Line* also putting in memorable runs.

The last original Pacific worked its last passenger train on the morning Salisbury–Waterloo commuter service on 5 July. On 6 July such was the spirited running of 35007 on the 17.30 Weymouth–Waterloo, where 98mph was recorded near Woking, that she suffered an over-heated big end but still managed to 'limp' at 60mph to Waterloo. But one run that deserves a more detailed mention was again recorded by Winkworth and coincidentally photographed by me when 35008 *Orient Line* was running near 100mph.

No 34025 *Whimple* is seen at Waterloo on the 09.33 excursion to Bournemouth on 2 July 1967 alongside a Portsmouth service comprising 4COR electric units. The 4CORs were built in 1938 for the Portsmouth direct electrification whereas 'WC' 34025 *Whimple* was built in 1946 and rebuilt in 1957. The 4CORs lasted another five years beyond 34025's withdrawal date at the end of steam. *KGV*

The train was the 18.38 Salisbury to Waterloo that set off behind Driver De'Ath of Basingstoke on 5 July 1967. He ran the 17.3 miles to Andover in 18min 15sec net, hitting 102mph at MP69 between Grateley and Andover, and then went on to cover the 18.6 miles to Basingstoke in 18 minutes. Here there was a crew change with Driver Aynsley of Nine Elms relieving De'Ath. He covered the 23.5 miles to Woking in 19min 15sec, achieving 98mph through Winchfield and Fleet. He had just failed to better Driver Burridge's run of 28 June 1967 behind 35003 *Royal Mail* of 18min 15sec when 105mph was achieved through Winchfield and 102mph through Fleet.

I am very grateful for Nine Elms fireman Les Greer allowing me to use this picture (right). Yes, you got it, it's a Bulleid Pacific speedo off the scale at 104mph! Les is pretty certain this was achieved downhill approaching Winchester but is uncertain as to which loco he was on. He had specifically thought it was light Pacific 34025 but an independent timer he knew well assured him he didn't exceed 90mph that day. So he thinks it is more likely to be on a 'Merchant Navy' hauling the 08.30 ex Waterloo on a Saturday in 1967 as he knows he exceeded 100mph with driver Jim Twyman. Apparently there was a whip round at Bournemouth by appreciative enthusiasts, presenting the crew with about £6 in loose change in the fireman's cap! The picture just oozes all the excitement of those last weeks and the sheer exhilaration that must have been felt on the footplate on those occasions.

The 'Belle' was hauled by steam on two days – 3 July with 34025 (see page 155) and 5 July with 34024 and 34036 in down and up directions respectively. Even the WR routes were affected with 34095 *Brentnor* working into Reading on the Poole–Newcastle and return diagram on 4 July. On the last weekday (7 July), some 50 steam workings, including station pilots, were recorded over the whole division. At Worting Junction I photographed some eight steam workings that evening starting with 34093 on the down 17.23 Waterloo–Bournemouth (FO) and 35023 on the 16.00 up Channel Islands working. The main catch of the day was to record the last up Salisbury steam working, the 18.38 Salisbury–Waterloo. This turned up behind 73029, the green Standard 5, and famously disappointed Driver Bert Aynsley waiting to relieve the crew at Basingstoke. He was hoping for a last fling with a Bulleid (having worked 35008 two days earlier) and his heart sank when he saw the Class 5 and

A Bulleid Pacific off the dial down Winchester bank... *Les Greer*

knew it to be in poor nick. He commented that he didn't manage to get her over 75mph on the greyhound stretch – 'the loco proved to be just as weak as I had expected it to be.'

The last weekend was to prove to be eventful. Early in the morning of Saturday 8 July the 04.05 Basingstoke down newspaper train behind 34095 *Brentnor* hit 94mph on the descent through Wallers Ash as she approached Winchester. The 08.30 Waterloo–Weymouth was not a steam-diagrammed turn and had not been steam all week. Yet, from those who worked in the Southern's Wimbledon office at the time, we had heard to expect this train to be steam hauled...and to be the last one. Sure enough, it met all expectations behind 35023 *Holland-Afrika Line*. It had an unscheduled stop at Woking to pick up a party of delayed enthusiasts who had been travelling steam workings overnight but had been caught out by a diesel service train failure. A speed of 94mph was reached at Winchester. And then, diagrammed or not, she had it all to do again on a return Channel Islands boat train to Waterloo. But this still was not the end. No 34037 *Clovelly* was recorded on a special boat train working to Southampton Docks leaving at 18.20 whilst in the night 35030 *Elder Dempster Lines* left on the 02.30 to Poole and later that day there was an up boat train from Southampton to Waterloo behind 34021 *Dartmoor*. But there was to be one more significant steam working. Despite the lack of success of

SR staff attempting to roster 35023 for the last down 'Belle', fate was to play its hand with 35030 again covering for a failed diesel on the up 14.07 Weymouth–Waterloo on the final day, 9 July. Apparently there was some confusion as to whether the loco would come off at Bournemouth but she succeeded in working all the way through. She ran a few minutes ahead of the Brush-hauled 'Belle' and was worked by Driver Hardy and Fireman Smith of Bournemouth, arriving 10 minutes early at Waterloo. As has been described in other articles, this loco, the last 'Merchant Navy' to be built, was the last loco to leave Waterloo and was at the hands of Jim Evans who was expecting to dispose of a Brush 4. In Bird's book Evans is quoted as saying '… we left Waterloo for the last time, giving plenty of blasts on the whistle…and we trundled slowly down the local line and into Nine Elms. I waited to watch as the smokebox faded from view (his fireman was now disposing of the loco) into the darkness of the shed building. There was a last mournful cry from her whistle, denied a full blast because already the steam of her life was ebbing away from the boiler, and then she was gone, absorbed into the blackness of the locomotive graveyard.'

The sheer speed achievements were remarkable from what was a rundown fleet of locomotives. But it is a comment in Winkworth's book that I think sums it all up. He refers to the plaudits the rebuilt Bulleids received, including one from no less a luminary than S. O. Ell of Swindon who rated them nearly as good as a 'King'. That is no faint praise from a GWR man. Winkworth goes on to note the remarkably consistent performances they turned in on a day to day basis whilst the speed feats achieved with an under-maintained fleet at the end had never been emulated elsewhere on BR apart from the specially prepared 'A4' in 1959 and the WR's attempt to get to 100mph on one of its six hand-picked 'Castles' in 1964. Bulleid and Jarvis plus all the traincrews deserve praise indeed as we recall the events of 50 years ago.

The SR had originally planned for up to five steam specials for 2 July but in the end opted for one to Bournemouth and another to Weymouth. Demand may have been curtailed by the seemingly high fare of £4 return. The two trains were to be hauled by 'MNs' suitably cleaned and with nameplates restored to the locos for this occasion only. As can be seen in this photograph taken between Farnborough and Fleet, 'WC' 34025 *Whimple* heading the 09.33 Waterloo–Bournemouth standard fare excursion was not so pristine as the 'MNs' that followed. *GPC*

Shortly afterwards, 'MN' 35008 *Orient Line* with nameplates restored heads the first of the SR's 'Farewell to Steam' specials. This was the 09.55 Waterloo departure for Weymouth which the loco would work all the way through. Here she is travelling at some 75mph and went on to achieve 88mph maximum during the run. *GPC*

'WC' 34025 *Whimple* has reached Southampton at the head of the 09.33 Waterloo–Bournemouth on 2 July 1967. Our intrepid photographer, Ken Vernon, has travelled down on this train so he can take photos of the following specials, unfortunately not over successfully as the results are impacted by some very dull weather at Southampton. No 34025 has just taken water before proceeding to Bournemouth. A youngster looks on as the driver, regrettably still unidentified, looks back down the train. No 34025 was to feature later in the week as a regular performer. *KGV*

Because of the gap in departures between the two specials, there was enough time to change location and get trackside before the second train arrived. 'MN' 35028 *Clan Line* hauled the second SR sponsored 'Farewell to Steam' tour, the 12.20 Waterloo–Bournemouth. She appeared to make an effortless breeze with her load as she ran on the down fast through Winchfield cutting with Nine Elms crew Driver Mercer and Fireman Dave May. Driver Robinson of Nine Elms is quoted in John Bird's book as saying '35028 was the best Packet…you only had to throw coal on and she would steam.' So a deserving case for preservation. *GPC*

No 35028 *Clan Line* gains many admirers as she waits at Bournemouth to take the return Waterloo special on 2 July 1967. The 'new' in the form of a Class 33 diesel just about to back onto an 8TC push/pull unit represents the future whilst on the same platform there appears to be a diesel waiting to head towards Weymouth on a four-coach train. Interestingly, having run only 794,391 miles and having received a Light Casual at Eastleigh a year earlier, 35028 was identified as the example to be purchased by the Merchant Navy Locomotive Preservation Society after their favoured engine 35022 had been condemned. Although 35028 was stored out of use at the end of 1966 she was repaired and put back in service in Spring 1967. She was only used once more in SR service, on the 08.30 Waterloo–Weymouth on 4 July 1967 plus a Weymouth–Bournemouth return the same day. *KGV*

The return train from Weymouth on the same day was to provide a rather splendid spectacle. Instead of a banking loco being placed at the rear for the 1 in 50 climb through Upwey, an additional 'Merchant Navy' was provided. This was an unusual spectacle as the pilot locomotive was normally detached at Dorchester. Here both locomotives, 35007 *Aberdeen Commonwealth* and 35008 *Orient Line,* are seen at Bournemouth before 35007 was detached for the onward run to Waterloo behind 35008. No 35007 returned light engine to Weymouth, her last working being the 17.30 Weymouth–Waterloo on 6 July 1967 where she achieved 98mph at Woking before suffering a big end failure. Nevertheless, she made it to Waterloo, albeit at reduced speed and making a momentous racket by the time she arrived. *KGV*

It is Monday 3 July and I manage to wangle a day off school as it was post exams and most of my 6th form compatriots were heading to the Hamble to go sailing. I had to make sure no one saw me from a passing train on the lineside! I had been advised that a number of boat trains were running that day and they would be steam hauled. I had looked at the OS map as I had always wanted to do some shots around the tunnels at Micheldever which, of course, had difficult access and treacherous lighting for the up workings. So I took an early train from Farnborough and ended up doing quite a lot of walking north of Micheldever station to get the lay of the land. But the walk was soon rewarded as I stood on an overbridge as 'WC' 34001 *Exeter* came into view at the head of the 08.10 Waterloo–Weymouth (Channel Islands) making light exhaust as she headed down grade towards Micheldever. *GPC*

There were two bonus days for sighting a steam-worked 'Bournemouth Belle' on 3 and 5 July. Just 31 years after the train was introduced by the Southern Railway in 1936, and with only six operational days left, we are fortunate to have 'WC' 34025 *Whimple* at the head of the 'Belle' on 3 July in both directions and Nos 34024 *Tamar Valley* and 34036 *Braunton* did the honours on 5 July. Here 34025 coasts down the 1 in 252 towards Micheldever on 3 July 1967 and is seen about to enter the Popham Tunnels, suitably compressed by a telephoto lens, with Micheldever station just round the curve on the other side of the last tunnel. Her last working was to be the 18.54 Waterloo–Salisbury on 7 July 1967. Built in March 1946 and rebuilt in October 1957, she finished her life with 872,938 miles on the clock. *Both GPC*

Only two original Bulleid Pacifics survived at the end of steam, though 34023 *Blackmore Vale* had effectively been retired as an appeal had raised £1900 for this loco in working order. Thus 'WC' 34102 *Lapford* was the only example to see service during the last week and here, in my last photo of an original Bulleid in service, climbs the 1 in 252 towards Litchfield Tunnel with mixed rolling stock making up the semi-fast 08.46 Bournemouth–Waterloo on 3 July 1967. Lapford would get the opportunity for a faster run on the non-stop Basingstoke–Woking section. No 34102's last workings were an up Salisbury–Waterloo commuter train and the down 11.38 Waterloo–Basingstoke parcels on 5 July 1967 though it is noteworthy that only two months earlier Clive Groome achieved 98mph at Fleet on the 18.38 Salisbury–Waterloo. Introduced in March 1950, 34102 had only run 593,438 miles at withdrawal that week. *GPC*

Not my finest photo but an historic one. The light was fading on the evening of 5 July 1967 but I nevertheless cycled to Bramshot between Fleet and Farnborough primarily to see the 18.38 ex Salisbury and the 18.54 ex Waterloo. Effective shutter speed was down to 1/60th sec so 'panning' was the only option to get a half decent shot given the slow film stock that I used. From this location you had to rely on sound as visibility was restricted in both directions. Sure enough I heard the pounding of a Bulleid Pacific and 'MN' 35008 *Orient Line*, devoid of its nameplates once more and with a mere six coaches behind, shot into view on the up 18.38 Salisbury–Waterloo in the capable hands of Driver Bert Aynsley, having something of a fling. He had taken over at Basingstoke from Driver De'Ath who had achieved the 'ton' before Basingstoke. With non-stop clearance to Woking, Driver Aynsley decided to give his steed 'a go.' The result was possibly the magic 'ton' at some point after having left Basingstoke at 19.24. Winkworth recorded 98mph through Fleet and this photo is taken a mile or so after so I reckon it is one of the fastest pictures ever taken of a 'Merchant Navy' – and in its last week! I was fortunate a few years ago to have Bert Aynsley sign an original print of this for me. *GPC*

8P

35003

Opposite: 'Merchant Navy' 35003 *Royal Mail* is at the head of the 08.35 Waterloo–Weymouth service on 7 July 1967 and has just paused at Southampton for water. This was the semi-fast relief to the 08.30 service that was diagrammed for a Brush Type 4, Class 47 diesel. Her last operational working was to be the 17.49 Weymouth–Bournemouth the same day. No 35003 had been a fine performer the previous three months. Keith Widdowson records her achieving six high-speed runs including three in the same week in April. One of the most memorable was on the 18.38 Salisbury–Waterloo on 27 April 1967 with Driver Chapman of Nine Elms at the regulator. She was recorded at 100/101mph three times at Winchfield, Fleet and Brookwood. Then towards the end, on 28 June 1967, 35003 was on the 18.15 Weymouth–Waterloo, comprising a mere five coaches, with Driver Burridge of Nine Elms and recorded a 106mph peak at Winchfield with 102.4mph average between Winchfield and Fleet. This is the highest recorded speed of a SR locomotive. Even without nameplates, the locomotive makes a magnificent sight – it is interesting to note that as I write this (December 2016) a '*Royal Mail*' nameplate has just sold for £38,000. If converted to 1967 money you could just about buy the whole locomotive for the equivalent price – Bulleid Pacifics had low scrap values due to their steel fireboxes being so much less valuable than the customary 2/3 tons of copper in conventional locos. The unidentified enthusiast in the rather formal uniform of jacket and tie was not untypical and though I considered cropping him out of view (taking the firebox with him), I thought it was of its time and should stay. *KGV*

BR Standard Class 4 2-6-0 No 76005 pauses at Poole on the 12.12 Weymouth–Bournemouth local service on 7 July 1967. No 76005 was a Southern loco all its life from December 1952 and was allocated to Bournemouth for the last two years. *KGV*

A standard view of Bournemouth...but it is 7 July 1967, just two days from the end, and here 'WC' 34013 *Okehampton* pauses for five minutes at the head of 17.30 Weymouth–Waterloo service. This was the last service working of 34013, a stalwart of both service and special trains. She was introduced in October 1945 and ran a total of 944,928 miles. Bournemouth station looks in bereft condition with roof panels/frontage removed along with the central roads too. *KGV*

Some 90 minutes later it's 19.54 on 7 July and 34013 crosses Battledown flyover, probably with Ken Vernon, our intrepid Bournemouth photographer, on board. It was so hard to believe that this was the last time we would see steam on service trains en masse. Being a Friday there were the usual extra FO workings so that in a space of little more than two hours, eight separate service trains were photographed, the last being 34025 *Whimple* on the final 18.54 Waterloo–Salisbury, which is a bit too 'thin' to reproduce here I'm afraid. *GPC*

The very last up steam working on the Salisbury line was on 7 July 1967 on the by now famous 18.38 Salisbury–Waterloo and which, much to the chagrin of Driver De'Ath, was diagrammed for the green Standard 5 No 73029. He was hoping for a 'Merchant Navy' to try and repeat the run of a couple of days earlier and later wrote that 73029 was a rather indifferent performer and struggled to achieve 75mph. Here 73029 is about to dive under Battledown Flyover. She remained in use until 9 July as she hauled the 09.47 Fratton–Clapham ecs working that day. *GPC*

Of course this shot is unthinkable today (and if honest, probably so then) but this was a last chance and I had no previous pictures at Worting or on Battledown flyover. But firstly we have that old stalwart 'MN' 35023 *Holland-Afrika Line* taking the elevated route over Battledown flyover at Worting Junction with the 16.00 Weymouth Quay (CI)–Waterloo service on 7 July 1967. No 35023 wasn't finished yet as we shall see in the next couple of pages. *GPC*

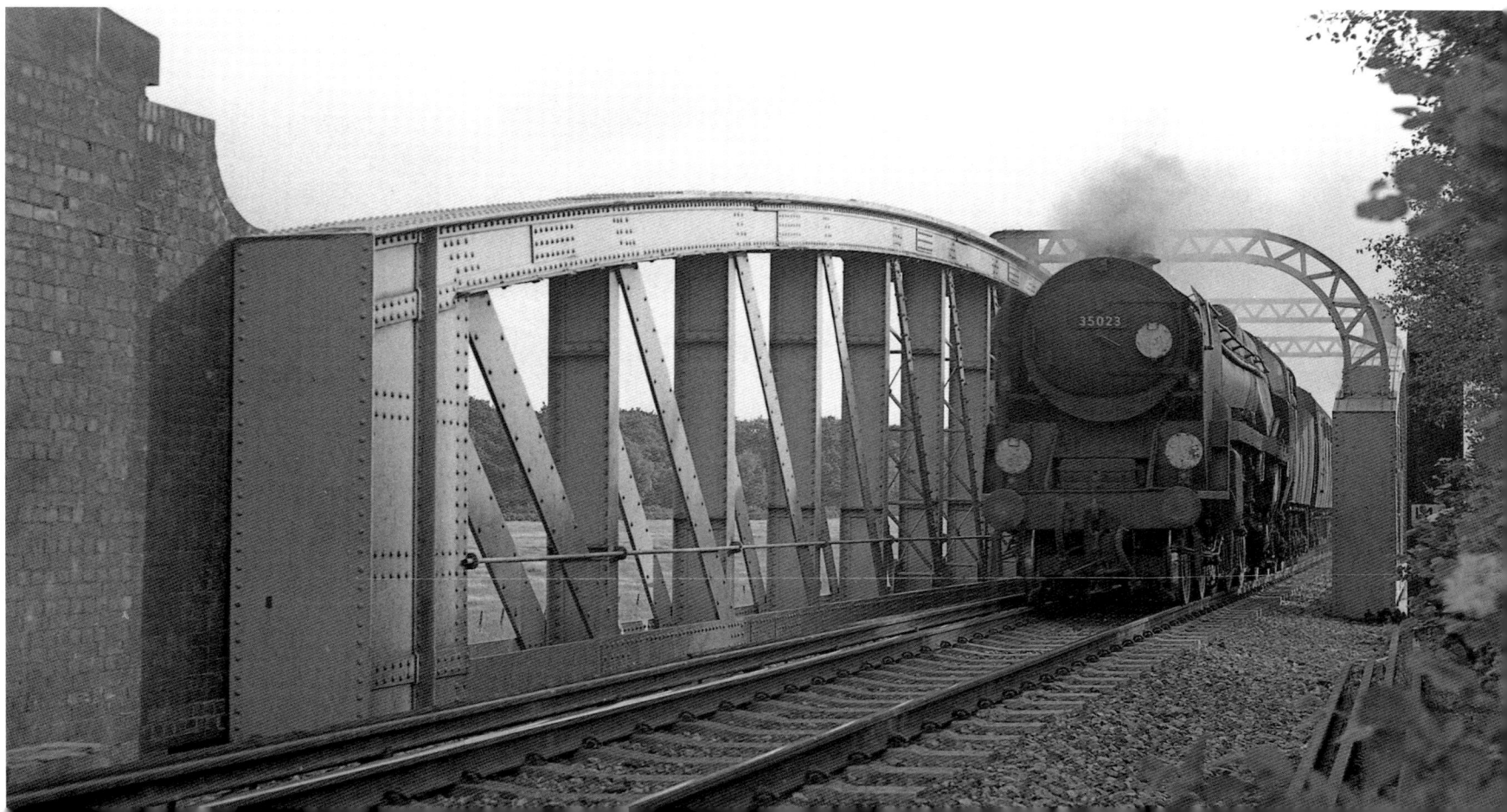

'MN' 35023 *Holland-Afrika Line* finds herself especially rostered by SR Wimbledon staff for the fast 08.30 Waterloo–Weymouth on 8 July 1967. The inscription on the smokebox says it all: effectively the last down fast working in normal service for a 'Merchant Navy' Pacific. She is seen hurrying through Farnborough station with the sun just giving an aura to the view with slight compression provided by a 135mm telephoto lens. The signal box to the right has recently been taken out of service with the introduction of the new multiple-aspect signalling. At this stage the locomotive is in the charge of the fireman/passed driver Alan Newman of Nine Elms who was also responsible for the inscription. He reverted to the shovel after a rapid run down the bank at Winchester and handed the regulator back to Driver Bill Hughes, both from Nine Elms No 1 link. The train was booked fast to Winchester for a water stop but a special stop order was issued for Woking to pick up a bunch of enthusiasts who had travelled overnight to Bournemouth but their return diesel-hauled service had failed. It was impossible for them to reach Waterloo but with sufficient connections to Control, they succeeded in getting the special stop order issued. Even with this, the service was three minutes early away from Woking and was soon up to the mid 80s around Fleet and achieved 95mph on the downhill stretch from Litchfield to Winchester. A fabulous finale! *GPC*

An atmospheric, semi-panned shot of the 08.30 Waterloo as she speeds through Farnborough in this view taken from the station platform. Alan Newman, who was previously paired with the legendary Bert Hooker, can be seen in the driver's seat whilst Driver Hughes takes a turn on the shovel. No 35023 worked the return 16.00 Weymouth–Waterloo service that day, ultimately running to Nine Elms shed to have her fire dropped after less than 19 years in service, of which 10 were as a rebuilt locomotive. Her mileage topped 941,326. *PJC*

Driver Bill Hughes and Fireman Alan Newman are photographed at Winchester City during their historic run on 8 July 1967. Alan Newman has just handed the driver's seat back to Bill Hughes. having been let loose with the regulator from Woking. *Picture courtesy Les Kent*

Slightly earlier on Saturday 8 July 1967, we are at Waterloo with the 07.18 Waterloo–Salisbury service behind Standard Class 3 No 82029 and the clue is that the clock is showing 07.42 and the train has yet to leave. This service was regularly diagrammed for a Standard Class 5 but for the last day, and a rather light train, a Standard Class 4 tank had backed onto the train. Pictures show it to be totally unidentifiable (see opposite). Fireman Jim Martin recalls that his driver J. J. Smith spied a Class 33 'Crompton' in the dock and failed the Standard 4 tank with injector trouble in the hope of a more comfortable ride. He was thwarted as Class 3 tank No 82029 appeared and was duly coupled up. Jim recalls that coal and water had to be used sparingly in order to run the distance. Ken Vernon travelled on the train and I wonder if he was intending to take the service to get down the line for the steam-hauled 08.30 departure or whether he was even aware of steam being rostered for this normally Brush 4-hauled service. The train was about 30 minutes late in departing but if he was aware of the 08.30, he could reach Basingstoke before it was due to run through although, with an 08.47 arrival, it would be tight. Jim says 'I don't recall a "packet" passing us' so maybe Ken was in blissful ignorance or just didn't get a photo – regrettably there is no evidence in his films of the day of 35023 on the 08.30 Waterloo. *KGV*

The Standard Class 4 tank, having been failed at Waterloo on the 07.18 to Salisbury, runs back out of the platform, light engine to Nine Elms.
KGV

No 82029 takes water at Woking...

... and again at Basingstoke where Fireman Jim Martin clambers back aboard 82029 as water fills the tanks. Jim recalls his driver had not signed for the Salisbury route so a pilot driver joined them. They took the loco to Salisbury shed and dropped the fire for the last time, less than 13 years after the loco entered service at Darlington in December 1954. *Both KGV*

The unique – to the Southern – BR Standard Class 3 2-6-0 No 77014 has just arrived at Bournemouth with 10.29 Eastleigh–Bournemouth on the penultimate day of steam working, 8 July 1967. The driver was also reportedly on his very last working turn and sported a top hat for the occasion and when detached from the train crossed the track to the shed with a cacophony of whistling. The following day 77014 was to head the very last recorded steam working on the Southern, the 20.50 Bournemouth–Weymouth vans working. The loco was then dumped in Weymouth shed and was still reported there on 14 August. It is a shame she was not preserved. *KGV*

Below: Rebuilt 'WC' 34095 *Brentnor* rolls into Bournemouth with the 10.13 Weymouth–Bournemouth service on 8 July 1967. No 34095 had had a rather remarkable working week, having hauled the 09.40 Poole–York as far as Reading and the return 10.08 York–Poole and thereby penetrating supposedly steam-free WR territory. However, she was to frustrate the ban again on the final day, 9 July 1967, by working the 10.20 Weymouth–Westbury tomato freight, one of three identical steam workings that day. *KGV*

Whilst an unexceptional scene, the combination of timing, background, subject and lighting means it is a 'must include' in this book. Ivatt tank No 41224 runs past the shed at Bournemouth on 8 July 1967. Whilst not recorded as hauling any service trains, this 'Mickey' was busy on station pilot work and was still in steam on the final day. *KGV*

The early evening sun makes this superb study of BR Standard Class 3 77014 on 8 July 1967 a superb valedictory shot of steam and its surroundings in Bournemouth shed alongside the coaling tower. The driver is even attending the locomotive in expectation of further work, which of course materialised on the following, final day. A magnificent portrait of the last steam locomotive to work on the SR. *KGV*

It is 9 July, with an almost cloudless sky. Rumours had been flying about a final bowing out of steam with a specially prepared 'Merchant Navy' being rostered for the very last 'Bournemouth Belle'. This was apparently vetoed by management despite the historic efforts of the rostering clerks. Many people had booked the 'Belle' just to be on the last run and in the hope it may yet be steam. Needless to say, they were thwarted but then a bonus occurred. No 35030 *Elder Dempster Lines* hove into view at Bournemouth at the head of the 14.07 Weymouth–Waterloo following a Brush Type 4 failure. Driver Allen of Weymouth was told to uncouple at Bournemouth, where a diesel would take over. But he was then told to re-attach 35030, meaning that a few 'Belle' travellers had to face the dilemma of deciding whether to take the bird in the hand and abandon the last up 'Belle' or wait in the hope that the last 'Belle' would yet be steam worked. I guess that with the down 'Belle' having been worked by Brush Type 4 D1924, unless that was attached to the Weymouth train it would have given some hope that the 'Belle' may yet revert to steam. But it wasn't to be. With 35030 re-attached and Driver Ray Hardy of Nine Elms in charge for the run to Waterloo, most steam enthusiasts opted for the certainty of what they guessed would be the last steam run to Waterloo. The photographer, John McIvor, was one such in this dilemma and opted to abandon his 'Belle' ticket for 35030, but not without first getting this rare view. I say 'rare' because pictures of this working, especially in colour, are precisely that. The train arrived 10 minutes early into Waterloo in the hands of Driver Hardy and as Jim Evans (whose last steam run had been 35007 hitting 95mph down Wallers Ash on 17 June) recalls, he had the unexpected honour to drive 35030, as the last steam loco to leave Waterloo, back to Nine Elms for the final fire drop – just 18 years and 3 months after entering service and having run a cumulative mileage of 850,876. *JLMC*

Postscript

I wanted to finish on the last up steam working for the main body of the book but it is worth just extending the story. I start off with the final 'Bournemouth Belle' on 9 July, which of course disappointed with its Brush Type 4 haulage.

The 'Bournemouth Belle' started in 1931, being hauled initially by a Maunsell 'Lord Nelson', and after the interruption of World War 2 was generally hauled by Bulleid Pacifics, primarily by the 8P 'Merchant Navy' class. There were a number of short interludes when BR 'Britannias', a Gresley 'V2' (when the Bulleids experienced a class withdrawal for axle testing) and the ex LMS diesel pair 10000 and 10001 were allocated to the Southern. It is a shame management would not provide the fanfare of a last steam working – perhaps aware of the potential criticism of the premium prices charged for the two official specials the previous week.

Above: At Bournemouth (Ken Vernon travelled on the last 'Belle' – I have his Pullman reservation and menu card) Pullman car *Aquila* – a 1951 BRCW built kitchen first car that was preserved – forms part of the 'Bournemouth Belle' formation that final day of operation. *KGV*

Brush Type 4 D1924 approaches Farnborough on the last down 'Bournemouth Belle'. *GPC*

... and is seen just 33 miles from final destination as the 'Belle' hurries through Farnborough on the evening of 9 July 1967 behind Brush Type 4 D1924, drawing a line under the train's 36-year career. *GPC*

On 9 July 1967 Standard 5s 73118 and 73155 head to Salisbury. *GPC*

Earlier the same day on 9 July 1967, the great transfer of locomotives to Salisbury commenced. This was to be the dispersal point for the steam fleet that was largely sold to the South Wales scrap merchants of Woodham's, Bird's, Cashmore's and Buttigieg's. On the day, locos were transferred under their own steam but subsequently were taken several at a time, in 'Crompton'-hauled freight workings.

Having photographed Standard 5 73029 two days earlier on her last passenger working, I also captured her on her last journey to the scrap lines at Salisbury on 9 July 1967. I then dug back into the files and found an ex works picture I took at Eastleigh open day in 1963 and then as 'luck' would have it my brother was in South Wales on a training course in April 1968 and thought he would just have a random look at the scrapyards and caught the scene of 73029 being torched at Cashmore's yard still with its chalk markings ('Play up Pompey'after Portsmouth football team). It is not a pretty sight but then, of course, with the next section of photographs we visit steam's saving grace, Dai Woodham at Barry, with a few pictures taken in the 1970s of Bulleid Pacifics and other SR locos that were subsequently saved for preservation. Although I doubt Dai was entirely driven by altruism, he earned the recognition he deserved in his role of ensuring so many steam locos survived into preservation.

In 1967 I had managed to submit some photos of Barry scrapyard to a national newspaper and they ran a feature for which they paid me the magnificent sum of £10 (Ian Allan paid 10s/50p in those days). I thought I would

Standard 5 No 73029 makes her last journey to the scrap lines at Salisbury as she passes through Farnborough on the down fast shortly after the last down 'Bournemouth Belle' had passed by on 9 July 1967. *GPC*

Following 73029's plight this montage shows her ex works at the Eastleigh Works open day in August 1953 and then the larger image shows her actually being torched at Cashmore's yard in Newport, South Wales on 20 April 1968 – note the Bulleid Firth Brown set in the foreground as Cashmore's scrapped many of the Bulleid fleet. At the time of this picture the photographer noted 34102, 35008 and 35030 being broken up with 34024, 34060 and 34089 awaiting their appointment with the cutter's torch – all locomotives featured in this book. *PJC, GPC (inset)*

have another go and cheekily wrote to Bill Woodham asking if he would let me photograph him with the loco line up. He agreed and I travelled by train to Barry on 1 April 1970. I still had a nagging doubt as to whether he would turn up but then a Rover P6 V8 came into view and he appeared. He let me interview him and take some pictures for half an hour. When I asked him why he had scrapped hardly any of the 200 or so locos, he simply replied – 'we haven't had time; we've been too busy breaking wagons which are easier.' Given the volatility of copper prices at the time, it might be argued he was speculating on copper prices but he had a large percentage of the Bulleid fleet with their steel fireboxes. History records that most of these locos were subsequently purchased and many restored over the following 20 years. Undoubtedly we owe Woodham Brothers a debt of gratitude.

On 1 April 1970 Bill Woodham looks towards original 'BB' 34073 *249 Squadron* which had arrived at Barry five years earlier and was ultimately saved. *GPC*

A line up that includes three original and two rebuilt Bulleid Pacifics with 34073 *249 Squadron* and 34028 *Eddystone* in the foreground. *GPC*

Bibliography

Books and magazines

British Railways Steam: The Final Years 1965-8, John Stretton and Peter Townsend, Silver Link

Britannia: Birth of a Locomotive, Philip Atkins, Irwell Press

British Railways Illustrated Vol 6, Irwell Press

Bulleid Pacifics, D. W. Winkworth, Geo Allen & Unwin

Further Ramblings of Railwaymen, Geoff Burch, Geoff Burch

Gradients of the British Main Line Railways, Ian Allan Publishing

In the Tracks of the Bournemouth Belle, Kevin Robertson, Crécy

Locomotive Compendium: Southern, Colin Boocock, Ian Allan Publishing

Railway World Vols 27/28, Ian Allan Publishing

Southern Steam Sunset, John Bird, Runpast

The Book of the Merchant Navy Pacifics, Richard Derry, Irwell Press

The Book of the West Country and Battle of Britain Pacifics, Richard Derry, Irwell Press

The Great Steam Chase, Keith Widdowson, History Press

Southern Region Engineman, Jim Lester, Noodle Books

Vintage Railtours, Gavin Morrison, Silver Link

What Happened to Steam Vol 5, P. B. Hands, P B Hands

Websites

Brdatabase.info

Disused-stations.org.uk

Semgonline.com

Sixbellsjunction.co.uk

Svsfilm.com (re Nine Elms Enginemen)

It's 1 April 2017 and it's no joke … Who could have imagined 50 years ago that we would enjoy the sight and sounds of five working Bulleid Pacifics on the Swanage Railway. Here, as dawn breaks, 'BBs' 34070 *Manston* and 34053 *Sir Keith Park* are being prepared for the day's work whilst Standard 4 tank 80146 simmers inside the branch shed. *GPC*

Phoenix-like, the Swanage signalman hands the tablet to the driver of 'BB' 34053 *Sir Keith Park* as she accelerates through her own swirling steam with an early morning working towards Corfe

Index of Locations